The book is really beautiful, and I feel en

— Conna Craig

I like the author's tools one can use to better their life choices and circumstances. It is a well written book, which draws the reader in with the author's ability to connect with her readers by describing her personal experiences. The author provides encouragement for her readers to take control of their lives and outlines the process of DIY conflict with proven professional results. This book helps you recognize your choice and behavior patterns while providing a framework to live a better and more successful life. No matter what your worldview or spiritual beliefs are, this author can help you be on your way to a better you.

— Theresa Buehlmann Steuri

Nance Schick has done a masterful job at identifying the many conflicts that affect our lives ... and to seeing the ways we are "conflicted" on a number of fronts. She also encourages us to challenge the assumption that tension and conflict always need to be the order of the day. The examples are clear and engaging (and sometimes, hitting a little too close to home), and the personal stories are compelling. The book contains practical, actionable tips to help us get out of conflict WITH conflict by helping us identify it, embrace it, transform it, and move on. I'm a colleague of Nance's who read earlier drafts of this book (full disclosure) — and I think that any reader will appreciate Nance's spirit of generosity and the clear, non-judgmental process she outlines.

— Nina Kaufman, Esq., Small Business Champion
and Founder of Business Exponential
(**https://businessexponential.com**)

DIY Conflict Resolution

Belle:

Keep shining your light
and helping others shine
theirs. The world needs
more of your eye, enthusiasm,
and art!

Best wishes,

DIY CONFLICT RESOLUTION

SEVEN CHOICES AND FIVE ACTIONS OF THE MASTERS

Nance L. Schick, Esq.

AVIVA
PUBLISHING
New York

Published by:
Aviva Publishing
Lake Placid, NY 12946
518.523.1320
www.avivapubs.com

Address all inquiries to:
Third Ear Conflict Resolution
310 East 46th Street, Suite 20G
New York, NY 10017
917.749.1631
www.3dearlisteners.com

ISBN: 978-1-63618-075-6

Table of Contents

PART II: MORE EXERCISES   77

Foreword by Dan Miller

Nobody really loves conflict and confrontation. However, it seems these relationship difficulties are inevitable parts of the human experience. With the uniqueness we are allowed to possess, it seems unavoidable there will be challenges. These challenges, when not handled properly, may prove to be destructive, demoralizing, and the cause of ongoing anger, resentment, and unforgiveness. Is there a process of sound problem-solving that can allow individuals to walk away from conflicts with their dignity and sense of wholeness still intact?

Fortunately, the answer to that question is yes. In *DIY Conflict Resolution* you will find the steps to a new way of approaching conflict. We have been conditioned to quickly jump to litigation—take any grievance to the judicial system. They will decide what is legally correct. But what about the human hurt, the broken relationships, and the damaged businesses that may be left in the wake of that legally correct decision?

I grew up as the son of a simple pastor who led people through the ages old wisdom of how to handle conflict; if someone offends you, go to that person and discuss it. If you can resolve it, that's the best solution. If not, take one or two others with you to get their input and make a clear case. If that doesn't resolve it, then go to a higher authority. In our culture today, we tend to skip the first stages of that process. We immediately jump to the overloaded, unemotional, and logical system to address a resolution, thereby missing the hurt, the fear, and the crushed expectations of the parties involved.

In this book, Nance Schick lays out a helpful, healing alternative called the Third Ear Conflict Resolution process. She encourages us to listen with our third ears, our h-EAR-ts, for the emotions that can be salvaged and healed when dispute occur. The cold formality of a court is frequently not the best option when human feelings are at risk. Perhaps we can learn this new way of listening well.

Understanding this process equips us for handling not only those inevitable conflicts with coworkers, neighbors, landowners, accident participants and family members, but also for the conflicts we have with ourselves. We frequently struggle with our bodies, our finances, our words, our mindset, and our belief in our own abilities.

This book will prepare you for a better, more congruent and productive life and to perhaps remove the necessity of ever seeing the inside of a courtroom again. As you work through the exercises you will learn to forgive yourself, forgive the world, free your emotions, clear your mind, and move forward with renewed boldness, enthusiasm, and confidence as you build your Third Ear skills.

You don't have to pretend that conflict will not show up. But now you will have the skills to create a positive outcome, no matter what the precipitating circumstances.

Nance brings a wealth of real experience to this topic. She is an attorney, mediator, and conflict resolution coach. She readily shares her own stories of conflict and combines her skills with her personal understanding of what is often behind the curtain.

You are doing something special for others and yourself – by reading this book! As you develop your own Third Ear, you will experience more confidence and peace – in your personal and professional life. And you will be able to share this powerful message that will inspire and encourage others along the way.

— Dan Miller, Author of *48 Days to the Work You Love*
(**http://www.48Days.com**)

Who Is This Book Written For?

I deally, I want everyone to have these tools. When I originally wrote this book, the news was filled with stories about conflicts—from Ferguson, Missouri, and New York City in the United States to Colombia, the Gaza Strip, Ukraine, and Mexico. There were rumors that terrorists were being smuggled into Europe among the Syrian refugees welcomed warmly by many countries, and the US Congress was threatening a shutdown. Not much has changed with respect to racial justice, ethno-religious conflict, or political posturing. People are still killing each other over religious differences, drugs, money, sex, oil, and other resources. Even when they aren't resorting to violence, many are verbally abusing each other on the internet.

We are still fighting in our streets, in our schools, in our homes, at work, and online. We haven't stopped blaming, demonizing, and expressing hatred or heartbreaking indifference toward each other. We think we are protecting ourselves and deterring future acts that we don't want to experience. Yet we don't feel safe or free, even when we "win" the arguments, fights, or wars. We need to take more effective actions, but we're not sure where to begin.

There is some good news. A 2011 Mercer LLC study of thirty thousand employees worldwide reported that as many as 56 percent wanted to leave their jobs. A 2012 Right Management study indicated that 65 percent of US workers surveyed were either somewhat or *totally* unsatisfied with their work. Then 2020 brought the global coronavirus pandemic, complete with lockdowns and remote work. Statista currently reports that 78 percent of US workers are now satisfied. That's a dramatic reversal.

A May 2020 CNBC study in collaboration with Survey Monkey suggested that high pandemic unemployment rates caused employees to reevaluate their views and expectations on work. We are making progress, in part through investments in employees, such as coaching, mentoring, and training. Maybe you're discovering what I did many years ago, after years of abuse and a suicide attempt forced me into therapy. Before then, I had no idea life offered more for me. I didn't recognize certain behavioral patterns in my life as dysfunctional, and I would never have guessed I could change them, much less the brain patterns that caused them.

I am more convinced than ever that we *can* have what we want. Over the past three decades, I have discovered many tools to help people create successful and satisfying businesses, careers, family relationships, hobbies, marriages, "sabbaticals," and lives. So this book is for you (and for me too). Nevertheless, I suspect that most of you reading this are high achievers who have gotten stuck in one or two areas of life. You might be an accomplished attorney, doctor, educator, manager, or entrepreneur with a solid career, but you are lacking family harmony, or you haven't found the partner with whom you can start a family. Perhaps you are an amazing spouse and parent, but you haven't been able to get your career off the ground. You've done all the right things where school, internships, and work experience are concerned, but you haven't gotten that big break to propel you forward into the Land of Success that you dreamed of.

You're not in dire straits, yet you're not exactly in love with your life either. You might even feel a little guilty about your discontent, knowing that there are many people in the world struggling to find food or clean water.

All these conflicts are normal, and you've come to the right place for building your skill in resolving them. In this book, you will learn to:

- Build skill in creating solutions from a broad range of options.
- Reconnect with your original and unmet expectations.
- Free yourself from anger, disappointment, and distraction.
- Discover how to listen for the real obstacles to agreement.
- Become the chief resolution officer in your life.

Am I a Conflict Resolution Master?

I prefer to think of myself as a master-in-training. As my extraordinary mother (a three-time cancer survivor) often said, "When you figure everything out, your work is done here [in this world], and I'm not ready to go yet." She must have figured it all out because she died in 2018. The rest of us presumably have much more to learn.

I discovered a great deal while writing this book and in the seven years since it was first published. That said, I do have what some people will consider sufficient credentials to be an expert in conflict resolution. I am an attorney, mediator, and conflict resolution coach based in New York City, where I have been in solo practice since 2003. I work primarily with managers and small business owners on workplace disputes, drawing from my pre-law experience as a human resources supervisor and employee relations representative. I was certified in mediation by the Equal Employment Opportunity Commission (EEOC) in 2005.

I created the Third Ear Conflict Resolution Program for a presentation I gave at the 2006 Southern California Mediation Association Conference at Pepperdine University's Straus Institute for Dispute Resolution. I didn't expect to write a book about it, but the presentation was well received. The more I used the process to help clients and loved ones resolve their conflicts, the more I applied it in my own life and new opportunities arose.

In 2012, I coached my first Self-Expression and Leadership Program at Landmark Worldwide, where I aligned with the Kaufmann Foundation on a project intending to develop entrepreneurship programs for the prison system. It was a lot harder than I expected to get into the prisons from this angle, but I haven't completely abandoned that project. There are just conflicts in and around it that still need to be resolved. When I was violently assaulted in 2014, I discovered more of them. It was that assault that led to the first edition of this book. I feared that the Third Ear Conflict Resolution process might have been lost, if my head injury had been worse, so I pushed through the post-traumatic stress disorder (PTSD) and other injuries to publish the book that same year. I also continued developing my conflict resolution skills.

In 2017, I was certified in ethno-religious mediation at the International Center for Ethno-Religious Mediation (ICERM) and served two years as the organization's main representative to the United Nations. There, I deepened my ability to listen to people with different worldviews. I learned that we don't have to agree with people to listen to them and that compassionate listening is among the most generous gifts we can give.

In this book, I will walk you through the Third Ear process so you can start using it in your daily life. I prefer that you not have to wait for the stressful environment of litigation to learn how to listen with your "third ear," or your heart. You'll learn techniques to deepen your listening to yourself and others, so you aren't as easily stopped by the occasional emotionally charged dispute.

I've been using the program to resolve conflicts for my clients, my loved ones, and myself since I formalized it nearly fifteen years ago. This edition includes updates on the original success stories, as well as some new ones.

That's probably what you need to know at this point about who I am and how I work. Rather than lull you to sleep with more words to make me seem important enough, let's get started in resolving some of the conflicts that are on your mind. If you want to know more about me, you can go to my website (**www.3dearcoaching.com/**) I've tried to keep it easy to find me by defying those who told me I should spell my first name with a "y" to look more professional and hirable after law school. The joke's on them because it's also good for search engine optimization (SEO). If you search for Nance Schick online, you will usually find me.

You can also find me on **Facebook (https://www.facebook.com/ nschicklaw)** and **LinkedIn (https://www.linkedin.com/company/ 34671371/admin/)**.

Make this your best day yet!

PART I

Third Ear Conflict Resolution Program

CHAPTER 1

Does the Third Ear Conflict Resolution Program Work?

I certainly think so, as do many of the people around me. I would not be sharing it with you if I were not confident that it can make a difference in your life. As a lawyer, I see too many people struggling, if not suffering, in ways that are preventable and reparable. As a mediator, I know what many still do not: There are private dispute resolution opportunities that often produce better results than a judgment or verdict. For this reason, I converted mediation processes into a do-it-yourself system: the Third Ear Conflict Resolution Program.

As you will see throughout the book, there is truly a lot you can do on your own. Yet we each have occasional persistent conflicts that we've carried for such a long time that we think they are as much a part of us as our height or eye color. We also have new conflicts that arise, with which we have little to no experience. These are the conflicts clients often bring to me with their requests for coaching, if not litigation.

My goal is to train you as thoroughly as I can—with an audio program, in workshops, and in other forms. This limits the amount of time individuals need for one-on-one coaching, while also preserving the funds you probably want to use for enjoyment of life. Not that coaching with me isn't fun, of course—especially when you get results like those experienced by Jan Rap, Omuk, Zhang San, and others you will read about throughout the book.

AUTHOR'S NOTE: *The names in most of the case studies have been changed to protect the privacy of people who have worked with me. I have also fictionalized some of them or their stories to further protect their privacy, and I have used placeholder names from a variety of languages to remind us that we all have similar, human issues. Our conflicts might manifest themselves in different ways and under different circumstances, but there is much we can learn from each other.*

SELF CONFLICTS

Jan Rap was a well-known and highly respected advisor to other professionals in a major metropolitan market. He was educated at private schools and studied abroad. He achieved bachelor's, master's, and juris doctorate degrees before gaining experience in a sizable law firm and eventually starting a profitable partnership with a more seasoned attorney. When Jan and I first met, I was a bit jealous of his success and uncomfortable being around him. He was dressed in designer clothes and was perfectly coiffed. He projected the image of success that I wanted but didn't yet believe I could have with my modest Kentucky roots and degrees from state-run universities. For a moment, I forgot that Jan was human.

Eventually, I remembered to use the Third Ear Conflict Resolution process to resolve the self-conflicts that arose in my association with Jan. I saw that I was discounting my unique experiences and credentials. I was valuing myself less than I valued him, when he was seeing me as anything but the loser I felt like around him. He valued me for our differences, as they gave us fresh perspectives. Once I started honoring myself and being "unapologetically me" during our networking meetings, we grew to be strategic partners and friends. When his business partnership dissolved, I cheered him along the path of sole proprietorship. When my mom had her fifth and sixth near-death experiences, Jan was there to hold me up.

> *Whatever our souls are made of, his and mine are the same.*
> —Emily Bronte, *Wuthering Heights*

Over the years, we became running partners and included our partners on our outings. (Jan is married to Fulan, a fitness instructor and actor who is like a long-lost sibling and who sometimes understands my musician boyfriend better than I do.) I created all of this by using the Third Ear Conflict Resolution process—made possible, of course, by Jan's interest and cooperation. We went from awkward would-be competitors to mutually supportive cheerleaders. So I was thrilled when Jan agreed to coach with me. That brought its own share of conflicts, which many people would have avoided and advised me to avoid. Yet we trusted the process and ourselves. When conflicts arose, we referred back to the Five Actions and took quick action toward resolution. It became another opportunity to practice our skills.

The first conflict we worked on was Jan's self-image. Much to my surprise, this strikingly attractive human being had his share of doubts about his physical presence. After being unable to create a family with his adoring spouse, he also sustained an injury in one of those embarrassing I-can't-be-this-old accidents. He had gained weight and lost fitness after only a short time enjoying the goals he worked for years to reach. His designer power suits that he once felt abundantly confident in now made him feel like "My Cousin Vinny"—at a time when his business revenue was down and his budget didn't allow for new clothing.

Most of us didn't notice Jan's struggles. They were subtle and, being the high achiever that he is, he was able to produce great results even under less-than-ideal circumstances. I began to imagine for him the results that he could create under better circumstances. He, on the other hand, was punishing himself for small disagreements at home, income shortfalls, infertility, and an ill parent with an uncomfortable, if not reluctant, caregiver.

We started small, and not because Jan's life was a mess—it wasn't. His clients were still happy. He was serving on corporate boards of directors and winning professional awards. His spouse still adored him, and they had a modest but comfortable life in their small home in an upscale neighborhood. He had friends, fun, and good health, especially as his injury healed. He just didn't *feel* like it was enough. I was honored that he trusted me with his secrets. We began with a small, manageable self-issue to build momentum and to avoid practicing on others and inadvertently causing new conflicts with them.

THIRD EAR TIP: *When we try to "fix" other people (especially when we are the only one who sees a problem), we leave them feeling broken. Don't "break" other people so you have someone to practice on. You have plenty of little conflicts in your life that will give you practice. There are exercises throughout this book and resources in the appendix to help if you have difficulty identifying conflicts in your life.*

First, we defined Jan's conflict with his self-image as succinctly as possible. I didn't need a lot of backstory explaining how he developed his current doubts. I knew many of the details of his life and, although they were interesting, they would have taken up time we could spend on playing with possibilities and creating a new future.

He laughed. "My body and I disagree about what a forty-something man looks, feels, and acts like."

Second, we identified Jan's interests in this conflict. We needed to determine what helped it take root, since nothing takes root in infertile soil. Sadly, he knew this too well.

We looked at his desires, thoughts, beliefs, expectations, wishes, and perceived obligations that nourished his tree of conflict so he could see it was just a weed. Then we could determine the best actions to uproot it.

"I want to be lean and strong. I want to walk down the street or into a room with my head held high and space to move around in my clothes. I want Fulan to look at me like I am the sexiest thing she has ever seen."

"I thought I had found the perfect workout routine. Then I got injured."

"I believed I would be a powerful, successful professional with great financial wealth by now. I thought I would be enjoying meals in five-star restaurants and taking vacations all over the world."

"I expected to have a family, a bigger home, and more money."

"I wish I could figure out what I'm doing wrong."

"I have to start seeing a return on my investments and making real money again soon. I am the breadwinner, and I'm not winning!"

Notice that the interests we identified were not solely about Jan's weight, fitness, or physical appearance. We went from a discussion of his injury and tight clothes to family and money.

Often when I ask people to do the above exercise, which is Action Two of the Third Ear Conflict Resolution process, they resist. They pretend that they don't understand the questions or the purpose.

They might even tell me it's a stupid waste of time and pout, sigh loudly, or grumble as they reconnect with themselves. I don't promise comfort throughout the process.

Jan and I made note of the other conflicts that appeared during this exercise, and we agreed to look at them in the near future. I assured him that they probably weren't going anywhere. Yet I also knew that as he gained more confidence and focus, he would start seeing shifts in many areas of his life.

Third, we played with the endless possibilities for resolving Jan's conflicts with his "aging" body. I reminded him that every body begins to age once it stops growing; it's not a sudden process that we wake up to in our forties and desperately fear. He was well aware of the diet pills, surgeries, weight loss programs, and quick fixes on the market. He had secretly tried some of them and discovered they were either scams or otherwise bad for him. Fulan would be disappointed in him.

We shifted his focus. If he could have his body conflicts resolve in any way possible, he would get back in shape overnight—physically and mentally. He knew this wasn't possible. His crazy-fit spouse was a reminder that he couldn't have physical fitness without mental fitness. Jan accepted that we had some work to do.

Fourth, we started creating a new future by developing an action plan that could fit easily into his current schedule, so that he could start taking steps and seeing results immediately. I am not one to postpone having a great life! (Most of the time anyway.) I coached him to set SMILE goals, which are a lot like SMART goals, but they feel a lot less like chores and a lot more like fun.

Jan's Specific, Measurable, Individualized, Likable, and Easy (SMILE) goals for the ensuing month were:

1. Eat green vegetables with at least one meal per day. To make this even easier while traveling or otherwise away from

home and the office, I recommended that he purchase some raw broccoli florets at the nearest market or go to one of the many Starbucks Coffee locations, which now carry cold-pressed Evolution Fresh green juices. (I'm not being paid to promote either business. I like sharing information that I think will bring value and ease to your life. You can also get high-nutrient, low-sugar juices in many other places.)

2. Incorporate more exercise into even his busiest days. There were days during which he had no time to go to the gym for a full workout, but we began to see the world as a huge playground with sidewalks for brisk walks, stairs for "mastering," scaffolding for chin-ups, and area rugs for lunges, jumping jacks, or yoga.

3. Look in the mirror and acknowledge one thing he likes about his body—as it is now—each day. This one was my suggestion, and there was silence on the phone line while he considered his arguments against this silly task. But he knows me well enough to know resistance is futile because I coach for my clients to win. Reluctantly, he took it on.

One month later, I was speaking to a happier version of Jan. He had even started to appreciate his injury and the "spare tire" around his waist (which was more like a bike tire than a snow tire!). He saw his injury as a symbol of an active lifestyle at middle age, and he saw his extra weight as evidence of prosperity: He had access to more food than he needed. Even if he bought some of his excess food on credit, he was lucky enough to be creditworthy. He also had some money in savings to cover lean business periods. He was in a much better position to succeed than he thought. He had just been impatient from comparing himself to other people he viewed as more successful.

THIRD EAR TIP: *It can be beneficial to look at others' successes for guidance in creating our own achievements. Yet no two stories are exactly the same. Don't look for a blueprint you can copy. You will need to customize it to honor your unique characteristics, experiences, and values.*

I still see Jan at least once each month at networking events. He continues to make steady progress, which I have since learned is consistent with his default personality style. A **DISC Assessment** (**https://nschicklaw.com/disc/**) revealed he typically has a Compliant style that is comfortable working behind the scenes. He will make quiet gains when he has good systems, which means he needs lots of time and space to tweak them as he and his needs change. Natural disasters, deaths of loved ones, and other obstacles have appeared, but he continues to return to his projects and perfect his commitments. He is less stoppable than ever before, and I am always excited to see his gains.

CONFLICTS WITH OTHERS

The Third Ear Conflict Resolution Program works in conflicts between or among people too. In fact, its roots are in mediation, a process in which a neutral person facilitates discussion of the dispute with the intent of creating new agreements that resolve it.

Omuk originally called me in search of representation in a lawsuit she wanted to file against her strategic partner, who refused to return intellectual property after their venture failed. Omuk wanted to rework her art and see if she could still release a finished product, even if it wasn't what she planned at the time she contracted with Zhang San. She recounted the emotional details of the situation rather than the facts, which suggested to me that the conflict was more about the loss of a key collaborator than the project. She still had a lot of respect for Zhang San's work, and she expected to see her at industry events throughout her career. I stopped her before she gave any specific evidence or opinions.

"It sounds like you still want this to work out," I said. "If you could produce the artwork with Zhang San, would you prefer that to a lawsuit?"

Silence. "Yes. I just don't know how to get her to talk to me anymore. It has gotten bad. We yell. She hung up the phone on me. Now she won't answer my calls."

With Omuk's permission, I called Zhang San and explained that although I had spoken to Omuk and had a vague understanding of the situation, I would like to serve as a neutral facilitator and create a resolution that would satisfy both of them. Zhang San was calm and agreeable. I asked them each to watch my **Introduction to Third Ear Conflict Resolution video** on YouTube to prepare for our meeting. After they had watched the video, they were to send me three possible meeting dates and times that they could agree upon. This gave them the chance to make a small agreement, which reminded them how well they could work together when they shared a purpose.

I got a call from Omuk approximately one week later. She and Zhang San had watched the video and started communicating more effectively. They began to speak about why they had decided to work together in the first place. They discussed their expectations and disappointments until they ultimately created a new plan for completing the project with what was still available. Omuk called because she wanted me to draft the agreement.

(Okay, that time it did seem like the program was magic! But it usually takes a little more practice than it did with Omuk and Zhang San.)

In short, the Third Ear Conflict Resolution Program works if you're willing to do even the parts of it you don't like at first or think are wrong. There is no right or wrong in conflict resolution. The goal is not to judge or punish. We are seeking effectiveness. What good is being judged as being right if you still can't produce results?

THE SEVEN CHOICES

One way to jump-start the resolution process is to explore and make the Seven Choices that I ask participants to make once they realize they are in conflict:

1. **Forgive yourself for having conflict.** We all experience conflict. In our relationships. With our bodies. With our finances. With our words. At home. At work. In our communities, and in our everyday activities. Punishing yourself for being human is a little crazy.

2. **Forgive yourself for hiding out too long and hoping that the conflicts would go away.** We all try to avoid conflict when we feel we can't handle it skillfully. We carefully avoid people or situations we believe might trigger conflict. We withdraw from groups, quit our jobs, and move out of our homes. We project issues with one person onto others. We become aggressive or passive, or we build other protective barriers. We live in denial, forcing our true feelings to find release in workaholism, obsessions, overspending, weight gain, or other addictions. Then we choose to take action and see results. Eventually we take action almost reflexively and see results more consistently.

3. **Forgive the world for having and creating conflicts.** Conflict is a natural part of living. There will always be conflicts we can't avoid, but we can choose to see them as learning opportunities or gateways to something better. There will be car accidents and traffic jams that make you late to a job you

The Seven Choices

hate anyway. The weather is going to change your plans—
and create a quiet night in so you can get a full night's sleep.
Not everyone is going to like everything about you or agree
with you all the time—because you're not really letting them
see you anyway and they know it.

Rather than pretending you can avoid all conflict, learn to
master resolution and whatever life throws at you. Isn't that a
much more powerful way to live? Imagine never hiding from
anyone or any situation because you know you have the
skills to create something useful under any circumstances.

4. **Free the emotions.** Many of us have been trained to deny our emotions so much that we can only feel them. We can't identify them effectively. Once we can understand them, we can allow them to pass through so they are no longer a part of the dispute.

5. **Clear your mind.** There is nothing but this moment...And now this one...And this one...And so on. Everything else is gone or not here yet—until you bring it into your mind. Did you just get something? Great! Now let it go. This includes assumptions—about me, about this program, about yourself, and about what you think you know.

   There is no right versus wrong, good versus bad, worthy versus unworthy, or anything along those lines. In the process of clearing your mind, focus on the connection that you once accepted wholeheartedly and rebuild it in a way that works under the current circumstances.

   No one has to lose. No one has to be punished—including you. Often, the dispute itself has been punishment enough.

6. **If you must make an assumption, assume that you know nothing about anything.** There is infinite knowledge in the world. You can't have all the answers. No one can.

7. **Listen with your third ear.** Allow your heart to open to the fear, pain, and human vulnerabilities of other people. Hear what every person involved in the conflict has to say. Get the specific details from their unique points of view, even if you don't agree with the ways they see the conflict.

Take a deep breath and try to enjoy the empty space you just created. Embrace a moment of silence. Be still. Don't be so quick to fill anything, especially not with things that decrease your effectiveness. Let's fill the space temporarily with a current self-inventory.

PRACTICE

- Take the **DISC Assessment (https://nschicklaw.com/disc)** and review your profile with me.

- List all the areas of your life in which you *are* effective. Do you do your job well? Are you a good cook, housekeeper, or parent? Have you developed a special talent or skill?

- List the qualities you have that make you effective in these areas. Are you loving, patient, diligent, educated, or something else?

- List the qualities you have that decrease your effectiveness. Are you anxious, impatient, lazy, self-absorbed, etc.?

- Review the qualities I asked you to list above. Answer yes to both sets of characteristics. There are times in your life when you have been each of them. They weren't permanent. They aren't part of you.

- Circle the qualities on your lists that you want to practice more often. Draw lines through the ones that cause you the most hardship.

- Tear out your lists and recycle them. (If you are using an electronic device, delete them.) You don't need them anymore. You got the insight, and you still know the subject matter: you.

- Do not continue reading this book for at least twenty-four hours. Instead, share with at least two people what you remember about your lists.

CHAPTER 2

How Does the Third Ear Conflict Resolution Program Work?

You have started to see the pattern in the Jan and Omuk stories. You might have even guessed what the Five Actions are. Maybe they seem simplistic and you remain skeptical. Perhaps you have life experience that seems inconsistent with my teachings. You rely on science, mathematics, rules, and laws to understand issues and to get results. So I did some research just for you.

Asking what quantitative research explains my results, I learned that behavioral scientists typically agree that there are key components to successful behavioral modification:

- Self-motivation rooted in positive thinking
- A limited number of very specific goals
- Practical ways to achieve the goals

After studying people who have successfully overcome addictive behaviors, James O. Prochaska and Carlo C. DiClemente developed the transtheoretical model (TTM) that is widely used today by psychologists, counselors, coaches, and others in transformational professions. That model considers the following:

- **Precontemplation.** What were the person's accepted beliefs or realities before he or she decided to take action?
- **Contemplation.** What are the key concerns driving the decision to take action? What are the actual, perceived, or possible obstacles to success?
- **Preparation.** What actions could be taken to increase the likelihood of success?
- **Action.** Which actions are or are not being taken and why?
- **Maintenance.** What environmental factors make it more difficult to consistently take the desired actions? How can the person eliminate or minimize those circumstances?

I didn't realize it at the time I created the Third Ear Conflict Resolution process, but I basically designed a program to reflect TTM.

THE FIVE ACTIONS

In Actions One and Two, we consider the actions and contemplate the beliefs, interests, and values that drove the actions.

In Action Three we play with the possibilities and potential actions.

In Action Four we choose the actions.

In Action Five we analyze them in light of the results we got.

Since I first presented the program in 2006, there has been new research on brain patterning and other neuroscientific discoveries. Addictions might soon be controlled with pharmaceuticals that change brain waves. Most of us can train our brains to be happy and to focus primarily on success. The brain is *neuroplastic* and can typically be molded into something that produces preferred results.

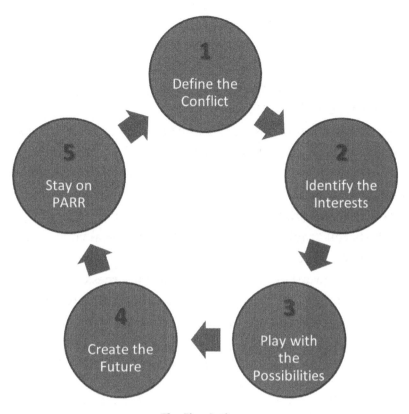

The Five Actions

My mom is one of the best examples of neuroplasticity I can think of. As I mentioned in the About the Author section of this book, she is a three-time cancer survivor. She had breast cancer that metastasized and attached to parts of her left lung in such a way that both lobes had to be removed in 1995. Her doctors prepared me for the worst. I moved back in with her, expecting to take care of her for the last two months of her life. She had a better plan. Rather than accept what the doctors believed was her prognosis, she assumed that we describe the work they do as "practicing medicine" for a reason (Action One). She chose to believe that they were making a best estimate (Action Two), but she trusted they had not mastered every element of saving lives (Action Three). She shifted her focus to generating improved health, and she saved her own life (Action Four). She has since done this two more times (Action Five). When she lost that focus due to fear or medication, we jokingly said I got full control of the brain we shared—until she could take charge again. She died in 2018 at the age of eighty-eight and with gratitude for her long, full life.

Author Hal Elrod (*Taking Life Head On, The Miracle Morning*) is another "medical" miracle who used the power of neuroplasticity to save his own life. After briefly dying on the highway after a head-on automobile collision with a drunk driver, he came out of a coma to news that he would never walk again. In a manner similar to what Buddhists call "radical acceptance" of what is, Hal chose to accept his circumstances and focus on what he could change. By not focusing on anger toward the other driver or the unfairness of his situation, he was able to see what my mom saw: The doctors were giving their best guess. They didn't actually know what was going to happen to him. He chose to try to walk again and has since completed not just a standard marathon but also an *ultra*-marathon!

THIRD EAR TIP: *Read Hal's books and go hear him speak if you get a chance. For more information, visit his website (http://halelrod.com).*

The effectiveness of neuroplasticity is not limited to medical issues. My mom's and Hal's stories are great examples of what can happen when our lives are literally on the line. Yet I prefer not to wait for a desperate situation. My vision is to have you living each day with gratitude and using your brainpower to create what seems impossible.

Nothing is impossible. The word itself says "I'm possible!"
—Audrey Hepburn

Erika Mustermann had been limited personally and professionally in many ways due to her diagnosis of bipolar disorder. She took daily medication to stabilize her moods and keep her behaviors within a relatively consistent range. Or at least she perceived her diagnosis as a limitation, and she was *supposed to* take the medication every day.

When we met, she freely shared her diagnosis with me and a few stories about her tragic life. Still, I could see how intelligent and capable she was. I did not believe that she was destined to reach only a level of success a few rungs lower than those without bipolar disorder. Erika didn't truly believe it either. I introduced her to several resources, including the Third Ear Conflict Resolution Program. Soon she realized that she disagreed (most of the time) with the limitations her counselors and society projected on her (Action One).

She wanted to be "normal" and have the same opportunities that persons without bipolar disorder had. However, she thought that she was disabled and different. She believed she was cursed or otherwise blocked from the life she wanted: a career (not a job), an adoring boyfriend, and a voice that influences the world. She expected to always be unfulfilled. She wished she were someone else. She had to live with her curse instead—or so it seemed (Action Two).

Erika didn't want to believe this was all there was for her life and, with some encouragement, she began to test her counselors and society in small ways (Action Three). She took courses that her counselors had discouraged her from taking, and she blossomed as a leader. She accepted new challenges at work, volunteered for projects outside of her comfort zone, and began taking responsibility for her physical and mental health (Action Four). With each achievement, her brain patterning began to change.

Previously, Erika's default thought process was to doubt, judge, and punish herself. She would also stop taking her medications, stay up too late, and consume caffeine to make it even harder for her to sleep. During those times, she figured that she wasn't able or designed to do much in the world anyway. So she would make her situation harder to overcome. But as she took new actions and started creating a life she enjoyed, she saw where she was creating her own strife. She accepted her diagnosis, but she committed to being no more limited by it than she was by her beauty, hair color, or height.

Erika Mustermann told her so-called defective brain to function more effectively. She made an agreement to take better care of herself and her brain to make the processes easier.

> *It might be that to surrender to happiness was to accept defeat,*
> *but it was a defeat better than many victories.*
>
> —W. Somerset Maugham, *Of Human Bondage*

Over the years, I have seen Erika dazzle audiences and handle new challenges with greater ease. She still has to manage her bipolar disorder and the occasional ineffective brain processes that we all have (e.g., "I'm not enough"). However, she is refusing to have less than the life she wants. She is staying on PARR: planning, acting, revising, and repeating until she gets the results she wants—no matter how long or how many tries it takes (Action Five).

There's still a lot for us to learn about neuroplasticity. I'll leave the scientific research to the neuroscientists and other such specialists. For now, I am trusting the results I have witnessed from the Third Ear Conflict Resolution Program and other tools.

PRACTICE

- Think back to your childhood or the childhoods of young people around you. Remember how Andrew sucked his thumb in kindergarten or how Liza picked her nose? Those behaviors were quickly unlearned and, in time, other disgusting or ineffective actions can be unlearned too.

- Remember how you used to have a habit of not cleaning your kitchen? Then the bugs moved in, seeking regular meals. Or you ruined saucepans that had been in your family for years. You trained your brain to notice and prioritize a clean kitchen. You can train your brain to process whatever you want, with practice.

- List areas of your life in which you would like to see more effective brain patterns. Do you keep hiring the same types of unproductive employees or dating the same types of unavailable people? Have you consistently made the same salary or been at the same income level? Do you hate going home for the holidays or calling certain family members because you repeatedly have the same lifeless conversations with them?

- Look for patterns that show up in many areas of your life:

Family	Friends	Career
I don't know how to talk to them about _____.	I don't know how to talk to them about _____.	I don't know how to talk to them about _____.
I don't know how to ask for _____.	I don't know how to ask for _____.	I don't know how to ask for _____.
I hate _____.	I hate _____.	I hate _____.
I love _____.	I love _____.	I love _____.
I wish _____.	I wish _____.	I wish _____.

- Brainstorm some new actions you might take if you had all the courage, skills, and solutions necessary. (This is especially fun to do with a friend.)

- Research TTM, behavioral science, brain patterning, or other programs that employ similar techniques so you can see their effectiveness. Some of the high-quality programs I am aware of are Alcoholics Anonymous, Al-Anon, Debtors Anonymous, and The Landmark Forum.

- Ask people you know and trust for input regarding the above programs or sciences.

- Trust yourself and give the Third Ear Conflict Resolution Program at least twelve weeks of effort before you resign to the life that isn't working as well as you would like.

- Join other Third Ear Listeners in the **online school (https://3dearlisteners.com)** and on **LinkedIn (https://www.linkedin.com/company/34671371/admin)**.

- Request one-to-one coaching on my **website (https://nschicklaw.com/coaching)**.

CHAPTER 3

What Is the Third Ear Conflict Resolution Program?

As I noted in the last chapter, at the time I created the Third Ear Conflict Resolution Program, I didn't know the psychology or neuroscience behind mediation techniques. I followed steps I was taught in my mediation courses, experimented with a few techniques from management and customer service training, and expanded what got my clients results. You do not need to memorize anything, and there will be no exam—beyond the quizzes life gives you. So as we move on, I again ask you to make the Seven Choices:

1. Forgive yourself for having conflicts.
2. Acknowledge yourself for taking any action to resolve any conflict.
3. Forgive the world for having and creating conflicts.
4. Free the emotions.
5. Clear your mind.
6. Assume that you know nothing about anything.
7. Listen with your third ear.

YOUR BRAIN PATTERNS GENERATE YOUR RESPONSES

You already have brain patterns that create your responses to the Seven Choices, which is why we are looking at them again and will continue to explore them throughout the book. They are part of the "contemplation" phase of behavioral modification, and they reflect the "precontemplation" phase in which you went about your life without a full understanding of how you choose your actions and reactions.

Many of us live in this manner for a long time before we realize that our experiences aren't simply happening to us without some contribution from us. If nothing else, we are creating or maintaining environments for them to occur. Jan Rap contributed poor eating and exercise habits to his life, which made it easier for him to lose the fitness level he wanted. Omuk and Zhang San contributed assumptions to their strategic partnership, rather than a written agreement or other clear memorialization of their intentions and expectations. Drivers take their eyes off the road for a "split second" to check their cell phones, change the radio, or reach behind their seats. Workers forget their safety equipment and choose to work without it instead of going back to get it and being charged with tardiness. Their supervisors fail to check safety measures or choose not to take disciplinary action. And then accidents happen.

We all contribute to our circumstances. Sometimes, the results are devastating. This is *not* a reason to punish ourselves, but we must acknowledge this so that we can see where to adjust. It is almost always easier to adjust aspects of our own lives than to force change on someone else. Yet we must also forgive ourselves so we can achieve—and celebrate—the best results. Making a behavior adjustment without self-forgiveness is like putting a cast on a compound fracture that has become infected. The injury won't completely heal, and you run the risk of causing greater harm. Again, forgive yourself for having conflict. You will get more opportunity to do this in the exercises at the end of this chapter. Likewise, there are exercises to help you forgive others and the world.

YOUR BRAIN PATTERNS GENERATE YOUR EMOTIONS

Brain patterns tell you how to deal with emotions—which is often to pretend you aren't having them, or at least some of the uncomfortable ones. You might have been told not to yell, which caused your brain to think you can't yell even when you are angry. Or you might have been told that big girls or boys don't cry. So your brain created a pattern that stops your tears from rolling down your cheeks when you are sad. Some people cry when they get angry because their brains signal tears to avoid yelling, and vice versa. Other people withhold laughter and expressions of love that they believe are unprofessional or inappropriate. It's no wonder we get twisted up in emotions we don't understand at times!

Since childhood, we've been repatterning our brains to respond to stimuli in unnatural ways. The good news is that we can still create new patterns. If you want to express joy at that, please do! You can let *everything* go that doesn't serve you, if you want to do so.

MY BRAIN PATTERNS HAVE GENERATED SOME SURPRISES

A few minutes in 2014 brought many opportunities for me to test my own program in my life. That will not change. There will always be conflicts we cannot avoid. We must use them to make us better and stronger.

TRIGGER WARNING! *This following story is explicit, quotes profanity, and might be inappropriate or upsetting for survivors of crime.*

The assault was violent.

I had just left the location where I had been learning to communicate more effectively. I had been there to create more effective solutions to some of our most persistent societal problems, and I was eager to share what I had learned. I called my partner.

As I often did, I called Peter when I was about two blocks away from the course location. I typically called to let him know that I was on my way home, that I was okay, and that I had new tips to increase our successes in many areas of life.

We were having a lovely conversation, and I was enjoying the mild weather between two major snowstorms. Ahead of me, I noticed a man crossing the street outside of the crosswalk to my right and walking toward me. I assumed he was drunk because of his unsafe behavior. He said something to me in slurred, unintelligible words. I thought he was either asking for money or had said something sexually disrespectful. Either way, I just wanted to get away from him. I did what usually worked. I moved to my left, intending to go up the street in the opposite direction.

He had a different intent.

The man grabbed my right hand, which still held my iPhone. I usually placed it back in my purse once calls connected, but I hadn't had time to do that.

I screamed, "Get off of me, you son of a bitch!"

It still shocks me that these words came out of my mouth. In that moment, I was probably angrier than scared, and I believed that I could break free from his grip.

I tried to shake him off, but he was strong. He must have recognized that I was too, because he went behind me and wrapped his arm around my waist.

I continued to struggle. At one point, I bent so far forward trying to free myself that my forehead tapped the top of the small shoulder bag I wore draped across my chest.

I tried to press my elbows into him at any angle I could, and I wondered why no one was coming to my aid—not the man operating the food truck on the corner, none of the other pedestrians passing. *No one.*

"HELP ME, PLEAAAASSSSE!" I screamed. Then the man picked me up from my waist and threw me against the concrete.

My head hit first, stunning me, but I reflexively held tightly to my phone. I had to keep the phone so I could tell Peter I was okay. I had to *be* okay. I was finally in a partnership with a good man whom I loved, and I was not letting go of what represented him in that moment: the phone that connected our call. I felt the earbuds and cord rip from the phone as soon as I was grabbed, but I knew the call was still connected. I knew Peter was still there, even more confused than I was.

My attacker climbed on top of me and tried to restrain me. I was immediately reminded of the sixteen-year-old boy who mounted my frightened, confused body at age twelve—and the friend who wasn't satisfied to sleep on my sofa years later.

I was not sure what would happen next, especially because not one person tried to pull the man off me. Regardless, I refused to be this man's victim. This fight, this time, would end differently.

He kneeled on my left leg and right arm, but I continued to kick with my right leg. He couldn't keep that position. So he stood up, grabbed my right arm again with his left hand, and opened my bag with his right hand.

I tried to kick him in the groin, but the baggy pants worn below his waist protected this vulnerable spot. I tried to punch with my left fist, but I was exhausted from the twelve- to fifteen-minute struggle, and I had not practiced this kickboxing move for several years. I completely missed.

He tugged on my bag and tossed me in such a manner that my legs, which had been directed north, were now pointing west. He must have gotten my wallet, placed it in his clothing, and tried to hold my left arm while he slammed my right forearm on the ground. But I continued to squirm and caused the wallet to fall to my right. When I reached for it, I slightly loosened my grip on the phone. My attacker grabbed the phone, stepped over me, and ran away. For a few seconds, I lay on the ground, defeated.

"They got him!" someone cried out as I was getting up, gathering the belongings he left behind and trying to orient myself.

Several other people yelled, "We called 9-1-1!"

A woman approached me and said, "Good for you! You fought back!"

Only moments before, there was no one near me but the young man on top of me. "Where were all of these people for the last fifteen minutes?" I thought.

"They got him—half a block from here!" I heard, and I instinctively began walking in that direction, not knowing what I was supposed to do or feel. Everything was blurry, and I worried that I had hit my head so hard that my vision was affected. Then I remembered that I had worn my glasses.

"Where are my glasses?" I asked as I walked tentatively back to where I had just been restrained and unassisted. I saw them approximately three feet from where I got up. A young man approached me and handed me a cell phone charger, earbuds, and a few other things that had fallen from my purse.

"It's 9-1-1! They need the name of the victim!"

"Do you need an ambulance?"

"Do you want to go to the hospital?"

"He threw her on the sidewalk hard! I saw it!"

"Good for you! As a woman, you have to protect yourself!"

Strangers were suddenly all around me. Some hugged me. Some filmed me with their cell phone cameras. One insensitive young man used his foam finger from a hockey game to steady his phone while he filmed the aftermath. I'll always wonder if he filmed the attack and withheld this evidence.

As I neared my attacker, the irony began to strike me. I had been attacked on my way home from an organization that seeks to empower all people to have great lives, including the man who attacked me. I was there to help people like him feel more powerful, yet he had seemed plenty powerful as he restrained me.

Less than half a block away, two men who claimed to be off-duty police officers had apprehended the man. He lay chest down on the sidewalk with his hands behind his back. My phone was above his hands and between his shoulder blades. Peter's name was still on the screen above the call timer. It read seventeen minutes and counting.

From the ground, my attacker said, "I'm sorry, ma'am. I'm sorry."

I ignored him. Someone told him, "Shut the fuck up!"

One of the off-duty police officers told me that he and his partner were in their car and on their way home from the hockey game when they heard my screams. They apparently couldn't see me because I was on the ground in front of a telephone booth and a food truck. But they saw my attacker run away and put the scene together.

I was grateful yet still in a daze. I said very little, merely watching the chaotic scene as if it were part of the evening news. (Later, I was surprised how common crimes such as these must be. There was no mention of it in the news. The videos never appeared on the internet. This scene that looked like something you would see on the news was no news at all.)

The other officer asked the assailant if he had a weapon on him. He said he might have a blade (a knife) in his pocket. I didn't see whether a knife was removed. I was just relieved he had not pulled one on me.

As I was listening to the off-duty officer and taking in all the chaos at the scene, I began to unravel. The officer reached out to me. He hugged me tightly and told me I was going to be okay. I began to cry a few tears and wanted to hide in his arms. Then I reminded myself to pull it together so I could give a complete and accurate police report. The thousands of fact patterns I had read and written in my law career gave me incredible skill in focusing on the relevant details and spotting the issues.

A mounted police officer approached the scene and disclosed that the 9-1-1 call hadn't come over his radio. He recognized the two off-duty officers and teasingly said, "I should have known it was you guys." They exchanged some pleasantries. Then several police cars pulled up, and the mounted officer left.

The off-duty officers ensured my attacker was handcuffed and placed in the police car by the uniformed, on-duty police officers. But I later learned that they didn't give statements, and the mounted officer pretended not to know them. Some former police officers and colleagues speculated that the off-duty officers had been drinking alcohol at the hockey game and didn't want to damage the prosecution's case with questions about their sobriety. I have wondered if they found and disposed of a weapon. Regardless, I was now safe and able to call Peter.

"I'm okay. I'll call you when I get home" was my immediate report, not considering that I wouldn't be going home anytime soon.

Peter must have been as shocked as I was. He responded with a simple "Okay." I quickly hung up the phone to protect him from the scene that was changing so much about my view of the city I called home. I wanted to sort it all out and call him once I was the same person I had been before the attack.

A female officer apologized that the only way to transport me to the police station was in a separate, marked police vehicle. I climbed in the back and sat where a prisoner would sit. There was less room than there was in the back of an average taxicab. I was uncomfortable, but mostly in emotional and intellectual ways. I could not make sense of what had happened. So I did what makes me feel secure. I joked, "This is the only time I ever intend to be in here!"

When we arrived at the police station, I was directed to a small area between the entrance vestibule and the detectives' office. I could barely squeeze my five-foot, five-inch frame between the bench and the table crammed into the space. Again, I was too uncomfortable in other ways to worry much about the physical discomfort, and I was afraid to take a complete inventory of my injuries.

To my right, I could see the captain's desk. It was much like the ones I had seen on television shows. It was wide and raised, like a judge's courtroom bench. It created an intimidating and authoritative experience of the officer in charge.

My assailant was escorted to the desk, where a brief report was given. I heard one of the officers say that the prisoner was fourteen years old. He had a prior arrest. His mother had been called, and she was on her way to the police station. I tried to imagine what that call must have been like for her. Who was she? Did she get the call at work, or was she awakened and shocked to learn that her son wasn't at home? Was she surprised and heartbroken, or was she angry that he hadn't brought home the cash she sent him to get?

As he walked past the room where I sat, I could see his boyish face. He was not quite the person who appeared as a grown man while violently restraining me and throwing me to the ground. This time, he didn't look my way. Yet I could see the wardrobe of a teenager: jeans below his waist, the waistband of his underwear showing a brand name, a hooded sweatshirt, and expensive name-brand athletic shoes. I began to worry what might happen to him in a jail cell or a prison. What is his life like at home that he was on a city street alone so late at night? Will his punishment be worse in prison or at home?

I wondered whether it was my fault. Maybe I shouldn't have fought back. Maybe I indirectly caused my own injuries by fighting him. Maybe I should have realized that he was "just" trying to rob me. I could have let go of my phone. It's just a phone. But it was *my* phone, a device I resisted buying because of its high price and only chose because it would make me more efficient in my work. It was one of the few valuable things I owned, and I worked more than sixty hours per week to have so little. How dare this "punk kid"—too young to work—think he can just take it because he wants it!

The longer I was alone in that room, the more my mind raced from self-blame to anger to fear to sadness to confusion to concern that I would completely unravel and never weave my life into the artwork I envisioned. None of it made sense, but what I did know was that Peter was always there for me. Even if I couldn't understand why or how, I knew I could count on him. I sent him a text message and asked him to meet me at the police station. Of course, he said yes.

Approximately one hour later, we left the police station in tangled, puzzled silence so thick that I knew almost instantly I would need professional counseling to restore my optimism, confidence, and self-expression. I didn't know that I would also spend months recovering physically or that I might have to live with chronic pain.

It's hard to believe it has been nearly seven years. The pain doesn't limit me as much as it did in the beginning. I no longer yelp like a puppy when I roll over in bed. It has been months since I've felt that pinched nerve sensation, and the numbness across the front of my left thigh is usually only a weekly occurrence. I am not running as often or as far, but I do occasionally run fundraiser races, and I've learned to swim. I've been told I already reached the peak of my recovery. Trying to prove the naysayers wrong has been especially difficult during the pandemic. But I am not giving up. Sometimes my stubbornness serves me.

I was advised to leave this story out of the book. It is graphic and might be more detailed than necessary. Yet I believe it important to express, as best I can relay it, the full range of emotions and thoughts of a crime victim. It has been a horrible experience for me, for Peter, and probably for the young man who attacked me. People have not known what to say and have, at times, made comments or asked questions that were unintentionally upsetting and even stupid. In the past, I might have avoided further communication with these people—at least for a while—and I would have cheated myself out of all the supportive comments and actions they offered. Because I could shift my brain patterns—even with a mild head injury and post-traumatic stress disorder—I was able to consider the true interests of my loved ones who sometimes suffered from foot-in-mouth disease. I created more effective conversations that kept me from struggling all alone. Interestingly, at the very time that I thought I might want to be coddled, I recovered my personal power and focus by leading discussions of compassion and forgiveness.

I even forgave my attacker. I held him accountable, but I also stood for his rehabilitation. I knew that hating him or harboring blame (of him, his parents, his environment, or myself) would not serve me or the world. Instead, I chose to focus on a happier, more successful future for us and the people around us. Throughout the prosecution, I repeatedly requested a Restorative Justice (RJ) Plea Conference that would allow him, his family, his attorney, me, Peter, the assistant district attorney (ADA), and maybe teachers or other authority figures to create a supervised plan for this young man's future as a high school graduate with no further criminal record and many opportunities for gainful employment, safe housing, and all the trappings of success. As I often tell criminal justice students, I quickly learned there was no such program in New York County at the time. That is fortunately changing, but it didn't change quickly enough for my young assailant.

It's not clear whether he was ready for a better life anyway. He pleaded guilty to second-degree assault, but he and his parents failed to appear for his initial sentencing. None of them could be found until the defendant was arrested on multiple new charges another year later. Because he was a juvenile, I can't track his case the same way I would an adult's incarceration. I can only hope that eventually he is inspired by the statement the ADA read in court on the day he was sentenced:

I am the lawyer and mediator you grabbed at 35th Street and Broadway. I am the woman you picked up and threw to the ground, where we struggled for more than 15 minutes. I am the one who, for the past two years, has dealt with physical reminders that I might not be safe in this city. I get that you might not feel safe, either, and that your world probably makes no more sense than mine.

There have been days in which I was very angry at you. When I rolled over, yelped in pain, and woke the man who had to listen helplessly as you attacked me, I sometimes hoped that you were hurting. I am sorry. I see that you are.

I have put those hurtful thoughts out of my mind because I know that hurting you would only cause us—and the people around us—more pain.

I'm sorry that I'm not here. I couldn't bring myself to see you this way today or to see the hurt in your parents' faces as they see you in custody other than theirs. Like them, I feel like we failed because of the choices you have made since your original sentencing date.

Since I learned who you are, I have been a stand for your freedom and rehabilitation. I trust that you have wished me well, too. You see, I know what it's like to be a teenager in a world that seemed to hold very little for me. By the time I was you age, I had been abandoned by my dad, neglected by my mom, abused by my sister, and raped by her friend.

I am not who you thought I was when you made me your target. I think you got that when I fought back. I was as surprised as you, because I haven't always fought for my life. I even tried to take it when I was 19.

I wrote a poem for you as part of my healing.

I Don't Know You Yet
—by Nance L. Schick,
Copyright 2014

I don't know you yet,
But I know you were born
With the same potential as I.

I don't know if you have
Two parents who wanted you,
But I know they love you,
Even if they suck at expressing it.
Mine did, too.

I don't know our friends,
But I know the people
Who put you in harm's way
Are not your friends.
Mine weren't, either.

I don't know who guides you,
Or if you try to do it all alone,
But I know you want
Something more than what is.
I do, too.

I want you to have opportunity
And joy
And love
And fun
And freedom.

I want you to be
Who you came to the world to be
To lead
To laugh

To love
To share.

I want to be what's possible
For you
For me
Through love
And courage.

I don't know you yet,
But maybe I do.

What I want you to understand is that your actions have an impact. On me. On your family. On this court. And on your future. You matter. So do all of us.

This sentence and your life are opportunities. Use them to make the world you want to live in. I don't think the violence is what you really want. You're capable of much more, and I want you to have that. You are not a lost cause. You still have choices, opportunities, and potential.

Please create something wonderful for yourself from them.

PRACTICE

- Explore an unforgivable error you made.

  a) What did you want to happen?

  b) What do you think you should do to make things right?

  c) What do you believe about such errors?

  d) Where did you get your beliefs about such errors?

  e) When and how did you choose to agree with these beliefs?

  f) What do you expect to happen to you now?

  g) What do you wish would happen?

  h) What do you have to do now, as a result of this error?

  i) What do you fear would happen if you forgave yourself?

- Consider an unforgivable error someone else made.

  a) What did you want to happen?

  b) What do you think you should do to make things right?

  c) What do you believe about such errors?

  d) Where did you get your beliefs about such errors?

  e) When and how did you choose to agree with these beliefs?

  f) What do you expect to happen to you now?

  g) What do you wish would happen?

  h) What do you have to do now, as a result of this error?

  i) What do you fear would happen if you forgave him or her?

- At the end of each day for the next five days, list every conflict that arose from the time you awoke and how you resolved it (if applicable). Acknowledge yourself for taking action to resolve conflict. You are already practicing!

- For at least one full day, allow yourself to (safely) feel and release every emotion that arises. You may do this in the presence of a trusted friend whom you've made aware of this exercise, or you might choose to excuse yourself to a restroom or other private area for the few moments necessary.

- Meditate for at least five minutes for five days in a row. (I'm not very experienced at this yet either. I like to lie on the floor in a comfortable position that allows my spine to open. Then I focus on the way my breath goes into my body and where it comes back out. I try to imagine that I can see where it fills my lungs and reenters the air.)

- List three topics you know very well, leaving five empty spaces between them. In the five empty spaces beneath each topic, add five aspects of the topic that you don't actually know as well as you think you should. Accept that there is always more to learn and be open to gaining a tip that might propel you forward in unimaginable ways.

- Choose three people in your life whom you would like to know better. Ask each if you can interview him or her to learn something new and to improve your listening skills. Assuming they agree, schedule a thirty-minute conversation. Questions you might ask include:

  a) What do you love about your life?

  b) What one thing would you like to accomplish in your lifetime?

  c) What would you like to witness in your lifetime?

  d) What do you think will be the biggest invention of the next twenty-five years?

  e) Do you get what you need from our relationship?

  f) Do you feel heard today?

  g) Is this new, occasional, or a regular occurrence?

  h) In general, or with me?

  i) What can I do better in my listening?

CHAPTER 4

How Can the Third Ear Conflict Resolution Program Work for You?

You are an amazing, unique creation. You are the only child of your parents who was born at the exact time you were and with the combination of cells, water, oxygen, and overall chemistry—if not energy—that you have. No single person on earth now or before has ever had this specific combination of anatomy, biology, chemistry, education, experience, genealogy, psychology, and sociology. Not in this moment. Never again.

Yet here you are, reading a book about conflict resolution, probably because you have conflicts in your life that have stopped you. I still have them too. When I was mugged, I became a New York City statistic. I have clients who don't pay me on time, family members who forget my birthday, and an occasional uninvited critter-guest in my apartment. I don't always like the outcomes of the court cases I litigate—or the ones I read about. Conflict resolution mastery does not make conflicts or disputes disappear from our lives or the world.

Let's choose again to not let conflict stop us from having what we want, regardless of our circumstances.

1. Forgive yourself for having conflicts.
2. Acknowledge yourself for taking any action to resolve any conflict.
3. Forgive the world for having and creating conflicts.
4. Free the emotions.
5. Clear your mind.
6. Assume that you know nothing about anything.
7. Listen with your third ear.

This time, in the clear space we have created, we are going to work through our first conflict together. Allow yourself to experience one of the conflicts that brought you to this book. It probably doesn't feel good or right. If you need to cry or growl, go ahead.

Forgive yourself for having the conflict. You don't want to be stopped, upset, frustrated, or confused, but there is nothing wrong with feeling these emotions or having these experiences. We make them a problem by resisting them or complaining, as if this will make them disappear. It won't.

> *I wondered if that was how forgiveness budded; not with the fan-fare of an epiphany, but with pain gathering its things, packing up, and slipping away unannounced in the middle of the night.*
>
> —Khaled Hosseini, *The Kite Runner*

Even if you are a recognized expert in the area where you are struggling, assume that you *know nothing* about the subject. You don't know how to "fix" it. You don't know who or what is right or wrong. Be open to reading and listening for new understanding that will lead to new actions and completion, or closure. You might even get a result better than the one you expected before you became frustrated, hurt, or resigned.

When my eldest niece was ten or eleven years old, she learned at school that girls begin to menstruate as they enter puberty, and that she will have this monthly chore forced upon her for thirty or more years. She was furious that boys were free from it. She did not want to grow up under such circumstances. She moped for days about the inevitable instead of fully enjoying her out-of-state vacation with her family. She still got her period many months later. Resisting and complaining did nothing but ruin the moments in which she brought her displeasures and frustrations alive.

That's how we are with surprises we don't like. We pout and mope, resist, and complain. Yet it doesn't stop the flood. (Pun intended.)

I was a master pouter. Ask my mom. It made things worse. As a child, I got teased and only felt weaker. As a young adult, I became withdrawn and isolated—until I discovered I could alter my experiences with alcohol. After a suicide attempt during a drinking binge, I started psychotherapy and learned to look at my world with the goal of freedom. Holding on to my past—no matter how much the stories justified my sad life or my stupid behavior—was causing the restraint I felt. Many books, seminars, and workshops later, I refer to my lifestyle as "conduitive living." I am but a conduit for the feelings, experiences, memories, and thoughts that flow toward me. I enjoy them as they pass. I do not block their path. I allow them to move on to nourish or alter what they need to encounter next.

> *How wild it was, to let it be.*
> —Cheryl Strayed, *Wild*

If you look at nature, you will see the beautiful way that life balances itself. In photosynthesis, plants take in carbon dioxide, water, and sunshine. They convert what they need and release what they don't into the air and soil so other organisms can grow from the excess. Likewise, animals take in food, oxygen, and water, converting it to the energy they need, and then they eliminate the excess. Even in decomposition, nourishment occurs. It's a complex life cycle, but nowhere within it is there an effective function of hoarding or stopping the flow.

Allow the flow of conflicts, emotions, and experiences to flow through you like the blood that flows through your heart.

Here is an exercise: Picture yourself on the gurney in the emergency room. There is a "crash cart" and a team of doctors and nurses around you. One of the doctors can be George Clooney from his *ER* days, if you want. This isn't as serious of an exercise as it might seem, and he's from Kentucky, like me. Enough said.

"Clear!"

It's time to defibrillate your third ear—your heart—and get you on a heart-healthy diet of listening. No more arteries clogged with anything. They are and shall function as conduits, just like you.

First, we must see what you think might be the problem. Like how you succinctly tell the receptionist why you want to see the doctor (when you're not on the crash cart, of course, and you're not), you want to direct your focus with precise language.

Action One: Define the Conflict

Conflicts with others can be clearly and succinctly defined as "_____ and I disagree about _____."

You don't need a recitation of the facts, whether they are "real" or perceived. (Most, if not all, of them are perceived.) You just need to know where the disagreement is based. Notice that the verbs used are in the present tense. This is intended to get you *present* to what is going on for you in *this* moment, not what you think happened. If you use past-tense verbs, you are likely stuck in the past and stating what you believe is a fact. You focus on what someone did, trying to persuade others that you are right. Remember, *there is no right or wrong in conflict resolution.* Release any assumptions, judgments, and desires to punish.

THIRD EAR TIP: *Conflicts with ourselves are sometimes more difficult to define. For a list of inquiries to help you narrow the conflict, refer to the appendix.*

Second, you'll need to give the doctor your medical history, and someone will gather data regarding your height, weight, and vital signs. We gather information to search for systemic conditions that make you function less effectively than you can.

Action Two: Identify the Interests

    a) When you put yourself in this situation or began this relationship, what did you think it would be like?

    b) What were you expecting?

    c) What did you really want?

    d) Could you still have that?

    e) How?

    f) What's stopping you from having it go that way?

    g) What new actions could you take to get a result different from the one you have?

Third, you and your doctor discuss prescription medications, diets, lifestyle plans, and other possible catalysts for a higher-functioning heart. You probably resist one or two of them and might even joke about a magic spell or an attractive doctor in your bedroom to jump-start your heart. That's perfect! This is supposed to be fun—so you will be more likely to use the process!

Action Three: Play with the Possibilities

Determine the ideal resolution scenario. If you could have any resolution you want, what would it be?

Fourth, you must agree to an action plan. You don't simply accept the one that the doctor gives everyone. You don't say yes to it because you want to look like a good patient (and later must lie about following the plan 100 percent despite the poor results). You agree to actions that make you SMILE (at least a little). They must be specific, measurable, individualized, likeable, and easy to incorporate into your life as it is now.

Action Four: Create the Future

Choose from the vast number of actions that could be taken and commit to taking three to five SMILE actions. I recommend that you write them out in declaratory language. For example, "I will _____ by (or on) _____."

Fifth, the doctor gets to play golf! You get to take action and share the results with the other people involved in the conflict. Or, if the conflict is internal, share them with a trusted advisor (maybe even your coach!).

If the actions taken were unsuccessful, review:

    a) What action was taken?

    b) Why do you think it was unsuccessful?

    c) What new action, if taken, would make it more successful?

Action Five: Stay on PARR

Plan, Act, Revise, and Repeat the action steps until you eliminate or transform the conflict.

You're not going to get the perfect result from the first action you take every time. But if you do what you say you're going to do, you will know whether at least one action produces the results you want under the circumstances surrounding it. You can either resolve the conflict with that action or eliminate it as a solution. If you do nothing, you can hide out and take your awareness of the conflict away, but you won't make the conflict itself disappear. You won't avoid the conflict. You'll simply postpone it—probably until an even more inconvenient time.

There is no better time than now to reclaim your power. Learn to handle conflict with confidence and skill, instead of pretending you can avoid it entirely. Commit to making and remaking the Seven Choices and stay on PARR.

PRACTICE

- Schedule time on your calendar to take your SMILE actions. For new daily habits, allow yourself at least six weeks of practice before they become part of your usual routine.

- If you are not using some sort of daily, weekly, and monthly planning system, experiment with different ones until you find something that works for you as your life is now. Don't worry about being "old school" or "analog" if it works for you. Your options include:

  a) An electronic calendar (e.g., Google, iCal, MS Outlook)

  b) Notebooks

  c) A pre-printed planner

  d) A desk or wall calendar

  e) A dry-erase calendar

  f) Something you create

- Schedule the time you need to complete the exercises in this book.
- If you are still skeptical about the program, use the process to:
  a) **Define the conflict.** Do you disagree with everything I have to say or specific techniques? Do you doubt the science? Do you disagree about our abilities to resolve any conflict?

  b) **Identify your interests.** What did you want from this book? What did you think you were buying? What did you believe about conflict? What did you expect? What do you need to do next or urgently?

  c) **Play with the possibilities.** If you could have this conflict resolve in any way possible, what would happen?

  d) **Create the future.** What actions can you take to have your ideal resolution become your reality?

  e) **Stay on PARR.** Continue to the next practice opportunity, and don't abandon this program until you have given it your full effort for twelve weeks.
- Ask at least three people who support your personal growth to hold you accountable for taking your SMILE actions.
  a) Give a weekly report on the actions taken, the results, and your assessment of your effectiveness.

  b) Ask for specific help in taking the actions, despite doubt, fear, time, or other obstacles.

  c) Invite them to join you in some of the actions.

CHAPTER 5

What If You Didn't Get the Results You Wanted?

If you got the results you wanted, congratulations! I am very happy for you and want to hear your story. Please share it with the **Third Ear Conflict Resolution community** on **LinkedIn**.

But don't get too confident yet. You will see quick results at times, like we did with Omuk and Zhang San. They will even come more frequently as you practice with the intent of mastery. Yet you will still have times in your life during which you will forget what to do next. Or you will think the conflict you face is just something you have to live with. You might start to accept (or have already accepted) that you are destined to be childless, fat, ill, poor, single, underappreciated, unknown, used, or worse. Or maybe your boss, child, parent, sibling, or spouse will always be cruel, irresponsible, self-absorbed, thoughtless, or unloving.

Ouch. Do you really want to resign to that life? Are you honestly willing to just toss away your power to someone or something else? I don't think so, and I am committed to you reclaiming your power.

If you want, go back to chapter 1 and make a current list of your areas of effectiveness. Then make the Seven Choices again.

1. Forgive yourself for having conflicts.
2. Acknowledge yourself for taking any action to resolve any conflict.
3. Forgive the world for having and creating conflicts.
4. Free the emotions.
5. Clear your mind.
6. Assume that you know nothing about anything.
7. Listen with your third ear.

Have you forgiven yourself for having a *recurring* conflict? Have you forgiven yourself for having this particular conflict?

When I was coaching Janina, I heard and saw her get empowered from the work we were doing together. She would go home to practice the process, and then she would return in a disappointed or embarrassed state. Sometimes, she would find excuses to skip our sessions, in part because she didn't want to face her perceived failures. Intellectually, she understood that she had made no new, special mistake that had never been made before by millions (if not billions) of people.

Janina had enjoyed a lucrative prior career and spent what she earned on entertainment, gifts, rent in an upscale apartment building, and vacations throughout the world. She wasn't notably wasteful and even took brown bag lunches to work. She was also financially generous with family and friends. However, she forgot to save for retirement during her prosperous years. When the 2008 financial crisis wiped out approximately 50 percent of what she had invested, she was left without a sufficient safety net. Fortunately, she was still physically able to work and create a new nest egg. That was what she was doing.

Tomorrow is always fresh, with no mistakes in it yet.

—L. M. Montgomery, *Anne of Green Gables*

Janina was quite responsible and typically did what she needed to do, both in our coaching relationship and in her life. Yet whenever she went home to the expensive apartment she shared with her husband, she would see many reminders of her (perceived) failures: invoices they didn't have the cash on hand to pay, her ill husband taking naps between work assignments, and trinkets from her late mother—who never told Janina she was proud of her.

Janina was easily triggered by those reminders and would hand them her power. She hadn't forgiven herself, and she kept focusing on one or two actions that didn't produce the results she wanted. She kept going back to fix them, instead of moving forward with the results she did produce. Her reaction is similar to what author Jon Acuff (*Quitter, Start,* also referred to as *Punch Fear in the Face*) refers to as "critic's math":

1,000 compliments + 1 criticism = 1 criticism

In Janina's case, it was more like:

1,000 good deeds

1,000 wise decisions

1,000 effective results

+ 1 error
———————

1 error

She wasn't going to forgive herself until she "fixed" her error and saved "enough" money for retirement. That seemed like a logical strategy, until we discussed how her error was actually a *perceived* error. I asked her to play with the idea that her current financial situation was exactly what she needed to create a new action plan. In fact, she didn't want to retire. She liked working, and her lack of funds allowed her to stay in the workforce without admitting to her husband that they had different visions for their later years. Or so she thought. Once they started discussing their wants and needs without all the judgments and assumptions, Janina learned that her husband also enjoyed the opportunity to work despite his illness. It helped him maintain a sense of contribution that felt threatened once their children were grown and needed him less.

Janina died at age ninety-four earlier this year. During her last years, she and her husband lived in a modest, yet comfortable home in an up-and-coming neighborhood. They continued to work and learned to enjoy the money left over for unplanned expenses or occasional fun. Even as her health declined, she found new ways to provide for her family. She maintained stronger relationships with other family members, friends, and former colleagues, which reminded her that she had been good, wise, and effective far more than three thousand times in her life. She began to recognize and laugh at critic's math. As sad as I was that she passed, it was a joy to see her create a life she loved to the very end. That is possible for each of us.

PRACTICE

- Schedule time to practice making the Seven Choices.
- Forgive yourself for having a conflict.
- Create daily affirmations and review them each morning, if not also before you go to sleep.
- List one hundred good deeds or wise decisions you've made (trusting that you've had similar effectiveness at least ten times more than you remember).

- List the ten biggest mistakes you've ever made. *No cheating!* If you learned something, took new action, and created something new or desirable in your life, it can't be on the list.

  Share with the **Third Ear Conflict Resolution** community (**https://www.linkedin.com/company/34671371/admin**) the number of mistakes you've made without learning anything useful. Write, "According to you, I have made ____ mistakes!"

- Ask your accountability partners if you forgot to include something on either list.

- Acknowledge yourself for taking any action to resolve any conflict.

  a) List the conflicts you resolved each day for a week. Did you fix a flat tire, clean up a spill, apologize for breaking a promise, follow through on a broken yet renewed promise, pay off a debt, return something you borrowed, or clean your home?

  b) Celebrate every conflict resolution in some way. Place a quarter or dollar in a container and save for a special reward in the future, buy a small treat now, ask someone to acknowledge you for your accomplishment, or take some time to nap, read, exercise, or do something else you enjoy.

- Forgive the world for having and creating conflicts.

  a) List ten things you wish didn't exist in the world, leaving three spaces between each entry.

  b) List three benefits of each of the ten things you wish didn't exist. Use the internet, if you need to, or ask your friends for input. Discover three benefits of each, even if you aren't the one getting the benefit.

- Free the emotions, and practice conduitive living.
  a) Let every emotion that arises have a release before the end of the day.
  b) If you are angry, call one of your accountability partners (who has no connection to the situation about which you are angry) and say, "I am really angry right now—not at you—can you listen and help me through it?"
  c) If you need to cry, let those salty tears flow until they stop. (I promise that they will stop!) Go into a private place, where appropriate. When you can, ask a loved one to hug you in silence until you are dry.
  d) Be mindful of your needs without trampling on someone else's needs—*even if you think they deserve your wrath.*
- Clear your mind.
  a) Meditate for at least ten minutes.
  b) Go for a solo run, walk, bike ride, drive, or hike—*without* music or the Third Ear audio program.
  c) For at least thirty minutes, listen to music without any lyrics and without engaging your mind in any other activity.
  d) Paint, draw, sculpt, cook, or craft.
- Assume you know nothing about anything.
  a) List five things you know "for certain," leaving at least five lines between each entry.
  b) On the five lines between each entry, write how you "know" each topic. Did you take a class, pass a test, or get a certificate of some type? Did someone acknowledge you as an expert on the subject? Did you see it recently documented or photographed? Is your knowledge firsthand or secondhand?

c) Begin to ponder what your life would be like if you forgot these five things or they were proven untrue.

d) Discuss this exercise with your accountability partners. Assume they know nothing about anything either. Don't be condescending or instructive. Open a dialogue.

- Listen with your third ear.

    a) Maintain eye contact during every in-person conversation.

    b) Ask questions to ensure you properly understand each point.

    c) Repeat or summarize what you believe is being communicated.

    d) Control your emotional responses (and release them responsibly when appropriate).

    e) Refrain from interrupting, correcting, or defending anything said. (This one can be difficult to master. I'm still working on it too. Don't give up!)

    f) When speechless yet compelled to speak, say something like, "Wow! I don't know what to say, except thank you for trusting me with that."

    g) Don't script or rehearse your answers, especially not in your head while you are supposed to be listening.

    h) Focus on hearing something new and insightful.

CHAPTER 6

Could Your Third Ear Be Deaf?

At this stage, you should be at your ideal weight, making more money than you ever dreamed possible, in a dream relationship or marriage, and surrounded by puppies and rainbows—with more pots of gold! Right? That's often how we expect mastery to go. Mamat was no different.

Mamat was a computer programmer and wanted clear, consistent results as soon as he identified any system error. If I had my DISC Certification back then, I suspect he would have scored high in the Compliant personality style, which is not unusual for computer programmers, lawyers, accountants, risk managers, and other systems people I work with. We spend a lot of time learning and developing our systems. We are attached to them. We rely on them. They help us feel more courageous and right. The problem is that people don't always function like well-oiled machines.

Mamat was in business with his spouse, and their skill sets were remarkably compatible for building a profitable corporation. With some of the revenue they generated, they bought the house they wanted, enjoyed hobbies together, and blended their families considerably well. From the outside, they appeared to be the power couple in their business and personal communities. They seemed to be happy and successful like Jay-Z and Beyoncé, Will and Jada, Dr. Phil and Robin, Oprah and Stedman, or Ellen and Portia. But Mamat felt underappreciated in the relationship. And we have learned how many of the relationships we idealize are as flawed as our own.

During a typical day, Mamat worked twelve hours, prepared the meals for both of them (and occasional guests), and did some cleaning. When he didn't clean, his spouse, Tipa, failed to pitch in and filth would build to levels that disgusted Mamat. Yet on four hours of sleep per night, he was too tired to effectively discuss what he needed or wanted. He told himself he would address all of it after the current project was complete. But there was always a big new project that followed and demanded equal, if not more, time.

Occasionally, Mamat would get several full nights of sleep in a row. He would take a day off to have fun with friends. Sometimes, he took Tipa with them, never hinting that he was questioning the health of their marriage. Then, on a day when he couldn't take the filth or (perceived) oblivion anymore, he would ask to have a conversation with Tipa. He would proceed to point out the "system errors" (Tipa not cleaning the house or sharing in meal preparation) and tell her how to fix them (clean the house). There wasn't much of a *conversation*. Mamat was trying to reprogram Tipa as if she were a computer instead of listening for what Tipa valued. Not surprisingly, Mamat was getting no results from his efforts.

"You are trying to install Windows 8 on a Commodore 64 and yelling at it to function like a MacBook Pro. How's that working out for you?" I asked.

He laughed. Then, he missed our next session. But I was too committed to let him stop pursuing the life and marriage he wanted.

When Mamat wasn't missing our sessions because he overslept after a long night of work or because he had a deadline to meet, we often talked about his marriage. There was clearly more than a dirty house at issue, and much to his dismay, the system errors were sometimes determined to be user errors. Here's how the dirty house issue played out.

Action One: Define the Conflict

"Tipa and I disagree about her role in keeping our house clean."

Mamat had not yet given a lot of thought to his role, but he did acknowledge that the house belonged to both of them. He agreed about sharing responsibility for the house, so I was confident he was also open to being accountable for the marriage.

Action Two: Identify the Interests

Mamat wanted a clean home and a marriage built on mutuality. He thought Tipa would take better care of the house since they bought the one she wanted.

He began to see that he had compromised and selected the house his wife wanted. Perhaps he was now holding her to a higher standard of caring for it—without sharing his expectations.

"I want the American Dream and 'happily ever after.' I got the degree. I got the wife. I got the money and the house. But I'm not happy."

Like a good mathematician, Mamat expected to follow the formula and get the result. He wished he had known the formula didn't always work and that the variables he needed to code around were unscientific and emotion based. He had to develop what many people still refer to as "soft skills," and he didn't like it. Yet he is one of the kindest, most caring people I have ever met. I thought that perhaps he was overcompensating, in fear of being seen as less than "a real man." The cultures that limit men in this way are doing them a great disservice.

Nevertheless, he started to understand what was truly at risk: his happiness. Despite the long work hours in isolation, the exhaustion, and the abandonment of hobbies he loved, Mamat didn't realize he was *un*happy. He thought he just hadn't achieved happiness yet, and that if he just worked harder, it would come like the degree, money, and house. Because Tipa was not a bad person, Mamat also avoided admitting he was unhappy. Tipa was smart, beautiful, and kind. Mamat loved her, and he didn't want to be divorced.

Before he attempted another conversation with Tipa, we tried to understand the range of interests that might have been keeping her from contributing more to housekeeping. We were careful to keep the language speculative, rather than declaratory, so Mamat would stay in inquiry rather than speeding ahead to a solution—before he had a true exchange with Tipa.

He jokingly said that she probably wanted a housekeeper. (That might have been accurate.)

"I assume she thinks a clean house is less important than I do. I like a clean house. It helps me focus on my work rather than all of the other things that need to be done."

"Tipa might believe I will do more if she does less. Of course, she wasn't that great of a housekeeper before we were married."

When asked if he had expected her to change after the marriage, he admitted that he probably had. But he wasn't ready to fully accept that he knowingly chose to marry a woman who didn't prioritize a clean house.

(Sadly.) "She probably expected a different marriage too."

"It seems like she wishes I would do everything."

"Maybe she thinks she has to rebel and show her power. That's not going to happen."

He resisted his reality. As much as Mamat said he loved Tipa, he wanted her to be someone else. He was adamant that he wanted to remain married to her, but he made her out to be a selfish rebel who victimized him. Having confronted my own stories of victimization and dodging responsibility for my life, I suspected Tipa was less of the cause for Mamat's unhappiness than he reported. Yet I know from my experience as a coach that the Third Ear Conflict Resolution process can be uncomfortable, as it disrupts our views of the world. I had to let him work through his circumstances on his own timeline, even if it meant watching him stumble a few more times before he created results.

Action Three: Play with the Possibilities

Not surprisingly, if Mamat could have this conflict resolve in any way possible, Tipa would clean the house—all the time.

I hated witnessing what I anticipated was going to be a journey down the proverbial rabbit hole. I doubted that a conversation from this viewpoint would produce the results Mamat said he wanted, but no one was in danger of harm. So I stepped back to let him try things his way. I should have known when his SMILE actions came with a scowl that we might be many strokes over PARR before we would see a desired score.

Action Four: Create the Future

1. Mamat would get at least six hours of sleep on the weekends so he could think clearly and listen attentively. (I urged him to agree to more days than two, but he refused.)

2. He would take at least a few hours off from work each week to have some fun with friends or practice a hobby he missed.

3. He would try again to talk to Tipa about the housework, and he would ask more questions than he made statements during their chat.

Action Five: Stay on PARR

Action Five was the most difficult for Mamat. His career training, education, and experience had his brain's default mode looking for a formula or a code to eliminate what he saw as a defect. Despite the science to support it, he believed neuroplasticity was inefficient and sought a quicker fix when our coaching relationship ended. When I last heard from him, he still wasn't happy, and he was managing his unhappiness with a baby on the way.

If equal affection cannot be, let the more loving one be me.

—W.H. Auden, *The More Loving One*

There's still nothing wrong. Not every conflict can be resolved at the time we first attempt to. Mamat and Tipa have a functioning marriage. Their business is thriving, and they've taken an occasional day off for fun with family and friends. They are surviving, and I suspect their child will force them to take new actions.

The Third Ear Conflict Resolution process isn't magic, and it requires full commitment.

PRACTICE

- Take a look at one of your "difficult relationships."
    a) What do you think the other person wants, thinks, believes, or expects from your relationship?
    b) Would you be willing to offer what you think he or she wants, if they confirmed your thoughts?
    c) Call the other person to find out what interests actually exist and discuss whether you can or want to offer what is expected.
    d) Trust yourself. Don't offer more than you can or want to give. There are some people in our lives whom we need to "love from afar" while we work through our differences. You don't have to cut all ties, but you can create new boundaries.
- Write for approximately ten minutes about your vision of how life would be if this relationship never changes.
- Discuss your vision with one of your accountability partners.
- Tear out your journal exercise and recycle it. You don't need it anymore.

CHAPTER 7

Could the Other Person's Third Ear Be Deaf?

Did you try to create a more workable partnership from a difficult relationship and fail to get a response, much less a result? I wish I could tell you that if you work at it long enough, even the most challenging relationship will transform. I can't. It would not be responsible for me to mislead you, and that is opposite of my intent. The fact is that there will be people who pass through your life, leaving little more than trails of litter—until you decide to make their garbage your art.

For Sarah, there was a team of "garbagemen" in her workplace. She worked in a small professional services firm where most of the women held administrative or support positions. At times, she felt like she was living in a season of the television show *Mad Men*. The hours were long, but the pay was great. It allowed her to drive a luxury sedan and buy a modest home in a popular neighborhood near her aging parents. She felt like a success story as she drove to shop for her latest designer suit and shoes.

Yet in the office, she was subjected to crude discussion of her work peers' wives or the latest woman one of the single men "bagged." Despite her disgust with the open bar and matching talk on the firm's so-called Team Building Nights, she did good work and made the owners a lot of money. She also made the group look more diverse than its mostly Caucasian male team with similar religious affiliations. I had met several of them and witnessed their disrespectful behavior, yet I had also seen them contain it and produce effective results. As much as I disliked seeing Sarah struggle to find happiness among them, I knew it would not benefit anyone for me to choose sides. My opinion would not create a resolution, but coaching, patience, and support could.

Action One: Define the Conflict

Sarah and her coworkers disagreed about the behaviors that professionals should exhibit in the workplace and the level of respect she should be shown by her peers.

I heard many stories about the conduct in and around the office. As a woman, I was sometimes angry, shocked, and offended. As a lawyer, I informed her that she might have a legal claim for gender discrimination. Yet from the lawsuit I filed against a former employer and the stories of many other workers who have filed claims, Sarah knew her life would be stuck in the past if she filed a civil action. Even if she could prove her case and win a monetary judgment, she did not want to stall or end her career advancement.

Action Two: Identify the Interests

A woman with an Influencing personality style, according to the DISC Assessment, Sarah wanted to make a lot of money, drive a nice car, live in a safe neighborhood, wear nice clothes, and pamper herself and her loved ones freely. She also wanted to be married, start a family, and do fulfilling work that was appreciated. (She had been about 56 percent effective in creating what she wanted.)

She thought the money and luxuries would bring her happiness. They did bring some.

She believed it would get better, that her coworkers would grow out of the locker-room talk and that she would eventually be respected as a valuable part of the firm.

She expected her performance and results to create more opportunities for her.

She wished, at times, that she had stayed in her prior employment.

She had to create an exit strategy that would allow her a smooth transition to a better job.

While Sarah was making plans, life happened. She got laid off before she had her debt paid off and sufficient funds in her savings account. She was in danger of losing her house, had to get a new car, and needed to support her parents financially. Yet in the wake of the rocking boat, she courageously worked through what likely happened.

Somewhat reluctantly at first, she considered that she was chosen for the layoff because her employer wanted to maintain a culture she did not like or want to embrace. She thought the overly informal environment was wrong; she knew that she wasn't a good fit for it.

She saw that her employers had probably thought the relationship would work out better than it had. In the beginning, she worked well with the owners and her coworkers, whom she saw rarely. Later, her coworkers began to complain about her lack of a sense of humor when their comments grew crude. They also viewed her as arrogant because she worked alone so much. They didn't realize or care that the more rejected she felt, the more she withdrew.

In frustration, Sarah said that her former employers and coworkers believed they had a good business because they made a lot of money. She agreed that they did well financially, but she disagreed about this qualifying the firm as a "good business." Again, their differing interests and values surfaced. It became more obvious why no one was happy.

They likely thought she would conform to their business culture. Most new employees did. The ones who didn't left in some manner.

Sarah said they presumably wished she weren't so ethical, sensitive, and strong-willed, even if they hired her with some of those characteristics in mind.

Finally, she accepted that they had to do what they thought was best for the business, just as she did. They might have even known that she was planning to leave and simply decided to choose her end date for her.

Many times, stories end here, or we read only the position statements of the parties involved. In their statements, each side tries to convince readers that they are the good guys. You are then given the role of judge or jury, and you're expected to choose who was right or wrong. Almost always, there were errors in judgment on both sides, or among all parties. Additionally, the relationships changed over time.

In this example, it might have made a difference for Sarah to know her wants, needs, and deal-breaking values before she took a job where she felt inferior and disrespected. Or she could have even adopted the crude behaviors of her coworkers and blended in with them (at least while she was at work). Instead, she hustled and found a slightly lower-salaried job with more manageable hours, doing work she enjoys in a more professional culture, in which she tends to thrive.

Action Three: Play with the Possibilities

If Sarah could have had this conflict resolve in any way possible, she would have found another job and left the firm where she was miserable.

She did find another job, and she did leave the firm. The sequence of events was just not what she had planned.

Action Four: Create the Future

Sarah had already been conducting a job search before she was laid off. She also did noticeably good work and built many loyal relationships with people who worked in and around her. She was out of work only a short time before she found her new position.

Action Five: Stay on PARR

When I last saw her, Sarah was *laughing*. She was learning to work with her new budget, and she was enjoying her reduced work hours. She wasn't as concerned about the pay cut as she thought she might be, and she was doing great work again. Sometimes, she even ran into her former colleagues. This bothered her a lot less because she was more rested, less stressed, and felt appreciated by her current employer and colleagues.

> *You don't have to live forever, you just have to live.*
> —Natalie Babbitt, *Tuck Everlasting*

The owners and coworkers she left behind are maintaining their status quo, and it is working for them. They thrive in their own ways, and there is no reason that Sarah and her former coworkers can't coexist. They just probably aren't a good fit to work closely. It's similar to how I see my relationships with my past employers or ex-boyfriends. We learned what we needed to learn from each other. One of those lessons is that we have incompatible visions for our lives.

PRACTICE

- Think of a past employer, lover, roommate, strategic partner, or vendor you are still bitter toward.

- Define the conflict: _____ and I disagreed about

  _____.

- Identify your interests.

  a) I wanted _____.

  b) I thought _____.

  c) I believed _____.

  d) I expected _____.

  e) I wished _____.

  f) I had to _____.

- Identify the other party's likely interests.

  a) I think he/she wanted _____.

  b) He/she probably thought _____.

  c) He/she likely believed _____.

  d) He/she seemed to expect _____.

  e) I suspect he/she wished _____.

  f) He/she probably had to _____.

- Play with the possibilities.

  a) Back then, if you could have had the conflict resolve in any way possible, _____

  _____.

  b) Now, you accept that _____ and would have it resolve by _____

  _____.

- Create the future and get this complete (or get closure) so you're not tasting anything but the deliciousness of life.

  a) List ten things you love about the past employer, lover, roommate, strategic partner, or vendor you chose.

  b) Call the person you chose (or a representative of it, if you chose an entity) and express gratitude for the contributions made to who you are today.

  c) Ask for an assessment of your strengths, weaknesses, and potential in the capacity you once served (e.g., employment, dating, cohabitation, partnership, business).

  d) Request forgiveness, even if the only thing you think you did was gossip, complain, or wish bad experiences upon them.

  e) Express forgiveness for what you perceived as a wrongdoing.

- Stay on PARR and get closure for other relationships that come to mind.

- Get coaching from me if you get stuck.

- Hire me to mediate the conflict.

CHAPTER 8

Will Third Ear Listening Make Me a Wimp?

Absolutely not and, in fact, quite the opposite! It takes far more courage to confront and resolve conflicts than to run away from them. Look around you. How many people are complaining about their lives, wanting change, and doing little more than changing the channel on television? Are the people who are calling you "soft" any more in control of their lives than you are in control of yours? Who do you want to have the power to define your life? Which makes you more of a wimp—taking responsibility for the results you produce and being in control of your direction, or allowing others to be the experts on your life?

By now, I have no doubt that you have started to see and enjoy some new opportunities for your career, relationships, and life. This might have caused some people in your life discomfort because they are seeing a more powerful, effective version of you. This does not mean that you will lose those relationships or that you must hand over any of your power. They are probably just as afraid as you were about making changes, and they need some time to adapt. They need to see that although some of your self-destructive behaviors have changed, you are still *you*. They also need to see that they can shift their lives in more powerful ways without huge disruption. Give them time, love, and patience. Use your third ear.

Action One: Define the Conflict

My loved one and I disagree about the positive aspects of my new behaviors.

Action Two: Identify the Interests

I wanted_____.

I thought _____.

I believed _____.

I expected _____.

I wished _____.

I had to_____.

Identify the other party's likely interests.

I think he/she wants _____.

He/she probably thinks _____.

He/she likely believes _____.

He/she seems to expect _____.

I suspect he/she wishes _____.

He/she probably has to _____.

Action Three: Play with the Possibilities

If I could have this conflict resolve in any way possible,

_____

_____.

Action Four: Create the Future

Create your action plan. Remember, you are the one who controls your personal power. You don't have to give any of it away. There will still be enough power for everyone.

1. Ask the other person about his or her actual interests.
2. Determine what his or her ideal resolution scenario is.
3. Negotiate a compromise that allows each of you to have some of what you want, if not everything.
4. _____.
5. _____.

Action Five: Stay on PARR

Plan, Act, Revise, and Repeat, involving the other person in your progress.

Do you still worry about being a wimp, or softening? How easy was some of the work you did? Some of your results were invigorating and propelled you into more action. Your insights challenged what you thought you knew about a core area of your life. These might have left you frustrated or fearful. At times, you might have ignored or destroyed your action plan. That's awesome! At least you made a choice. Choosing to take no action is still a choice, and you can always choose to begin again.

THIRD EAR TIP: *The only way to get someplace new is to start moving.*

You're not finished yet, and there will be some new challenges ahead. You will be tackling them head-on and moving toward the end zone, where you will accumulate points toward winning the game of your life—which you are designing. There is nothing wimpy about that!

I prefer that you not wait to begin again. If you are stuck in any area of your life, choose right now to take new actions. You got stopped, but you're not dead. There are numerous actions you can take to improve any situation.

Do you hate your government?

- Vote, assist campaigns, write to your representatives, run for office, or, on election days, help register or educate voters and get them to the polls.
- Play the "One Hundred Things I Love About..." game and list what you love about your governing bodies, laws, and systems.
- Share your list with your accountability partners or other people who might be inspired by it.

Do you want more money?

- Explore your beliefs, get another job, register to sell products through network marketing, sell stuff you own but aren't using, pay off any credit card debt you have (and save that monthly interest charge), or ask for a raise or other money.
- Play the "One Hundred Days of Enough" game. List one hundred things you've had enough money to buy.
- Share your list.

Do you want to change your dating status?

- Resolve any past partnership issues that still get you emotionally charged.
- Write your vision for who you are when you're in a compatible partnership.
- List and share "One Hundred Things I Love About…" your current partnership status.

Do you want a new job or career?

- Rebuild any bridges that you have burned.
- Give 100 percent effort in your current position (even if your current job is to look for a position in your industry of choice).
- Get feedback on your performance in your present job.
- Update your résumé *and* cover letters.
- List and share "One Hundred Things I Love About…" your current employment situation.

If you want to be anywhere other than where you are, you must start moving. The universe is in perpetual motion, but that's not enough to get you anywhere other than where you are. It's time to stop pretending someone took your power and left you on the sofa (or at your desk) with some mediocre life not meant for you.

- Be **S**pecific.
- **M**easure your results (but don't stare so long at the scoreboard that you forget to get in the game).
- Create an **I**ndividualized action plan that works with your beliefs, interests, and values
- Choose actions you **L**ike and that are **E**asy to incorporate into your life as it is now.

Do you want more practice?

- Use the tools in the appendix.
- Request a workshop for your organization.
- Apply for one-on-one coaching with me.
- Create a book study or practice group.
- Join my online communities.
- Tell me what else you would like to see.
- Let me know if you didn't get what you needed from this book.

PART II

More Exercises

I included practice exercises at the end of each chapter to help you better understand the material and to help you break through some obstacles immediately. Mastery is going to take time. For both of us. There will be periods of great progress, followed by occasional upsets. You will likely get frustrated now and then, forgetting you have tools to work through the conflicts. That is completely normal. As financial guru Robert Kiyosaki says, "When emotions go up, intelligence goes down."

Sometimes, I forget what I know, too, especially when I am emotionally charged. Fortunately, the decrease in intelligence is only temporary. It also lasts for shorter periods the more I practice my skills. What once derailed me for weeks might now resolve in hours, especially after a walk and a good night's sleep.

On the following pages are exercises from the audio program I began a few years ago. I had my own conflicts around it because it wasn't an instant success. I have since remembered that *it takes a long time to become an overnight success*. Another financial guru, Dave Ramsey, said, "I have worked my butt off for 25 years...now I am 'An Overnight Success'."

In other words, we don't see all the work that goes on behind the scenes before the curtain comes up, the cameras start filming, or the puck is dropped. We only pay attention to the results we see, and we do ourselves a disservice by focusing too much on them.

Our brains play tricks on us, but they can be rewired to work for us instead of against us. These additional exercises will help.

Resolving Conflicts with Yourself

Common feedback I get about this book is the readers' surprise to learn how much of the work that needs to be done is on ourselves. Yes. You are the common denominator in all your conflicts. Don't let that be an excuse to treat yourself poorly. We all have this basic conflict. Fortunately, we can also build skill in managing it. These first few exercises will help.

LIFE VISION CONFLICTS

(Listen to this sample exercise on Soundcloud. (https://sound-cloud.com/nance-l-schick/resolving-life-vision-conflicts))

Think back to what you wanted to be when you grew up. Sure, some of our childhood dreams were incompatible with who we are now and were rightfully abandoned, but what is it you wish you had tried? Did you try and fail? Did you give up too soon? Did you choose a different path because you didn't know what else to do, followed someone else's advice or thought it was "the right thing to do"? Or are you living the life you always imagined? Has it met or exceeded your expectations?

Some of my favorite authors (who are often mentioned on my **website (https://nschicklaw.com)** and **LinkedIn (www.linkedin.com/company/34671371/admin)** page) remind us that we are not here to suffer but to live, love, and enjoy our lives. If that is not the experience you are having, you have the power to create something else. However, you have to first be willing to look deeply into what you have. Then, you have to be willing to let it go if it's not working, regardless of how long it has been a part of your life. This is what I call "Conduitive Living."

Conduitive Living is based on what appears to be a more natural way of being than how most of us are taught to be. We are trained to gather as many resources as we can and to hold onto them for our survival. We do this (or at least try to do this) with food, friends, knowledge, love, money, and stuff: belongings so insignificant to our survival that we use a generic term to describe them in one big lump. Yet if you look all around you, you will see that most everything in nature is designed to take in only what is needed and to release what is left. We breathe in, use the oxygen we need, and release the rest back into the atmosphere. We eat and drink, process what we need, and eliminate what we don't. When our bodies don't or can't allow the waste to pass through, we develop illnesses—or worse. We suffocate, choke. or die.

Likewise, photosynthesis is a process by which the sun and water is converted to nourish plants. There are business life cycles, as well as life cycles for more tangible living creatures. Even our knowledge has a life cycle. For example, lying in bed and screaming until someone brings you what you need becomes a less-effective form of communication as we develop new skills. In the Third Ear Conflict Resolution program, it is my intent to remove any blockages in your life cycle so you can be most effective in your communication and creating the life you want. We start with your Life Vision because without some sort of image of what you want your life to look like, you will have a difficult time creating it—or recognizing it when you have it.

Look at who you are now and how you define yourself. Write down the first thing that comes to mind when I read the following statement.

I became a _____ because I thought it would _____.
For example:

1. **Define the conflict.** I became a lawyer because I thought it would put me in a better position to help my family financially. Don't edit yourself. No one but you ever has to see what you wrote, but you have to be honest with yourself to get to the root of a conflict. Don't assume there is a right answer. Don't judge yourself. Release any desire to punish yourself for your choices. You made them for what we'll call "good reasons," which are really your interests. In my example:

2. **Identify the interests.** I wanted to be more financially secure. I expected to make more money than I do. I hoped I could contribute something meaningful to society. Even if I doubt my choices or they aren't quite working out the way I planned, I had my "good reasons" for doing what I did. Rather than focusing on what I didn't do or maybe should have done, I need to deal with what is. Buddhists refer to this as "radical acceptance," which I love and find slightly humorous because it is pretty radical for we humans to accept what is instead of getting attached to what was or what we hope will be. Perhaps we forget that we created what is and would prefer not to take responsibility for that. Regardless...

3. **Play with the Possibilities.** If I could have this conflict resolve in any way possible, I would have a career that

allowed me to contribute to my family and the world both financially and spiritually. I might not have the entire plan mapped out, but after declaring this potential outcome, I see that it is still possible—if I am willing to take actions different from those that have me in the conflict. In other words, I acknowledge that the only way out of anything is to move. So…

4. **Create the Future.** Beginning today, I will review my finances critically and weekly. I will obtain expert guidance, as necessary. I will research actual attorney salaries, not the statistics advertised by law schools. I will continue to share my Third Ear Conflict Resolution Program. I will interview 12 other attorneys, including six who have taken non-traditional career paths.

Now, it's your turn to complete this exercise. What specific, measurable, individualized, likable, and easy (or SMILE) actions will you take to fulfill on your vision for your career, your life, or your latest project? Make a list of three to five steps you will take. Then, put them into your calendar and ensure you have allowed time to complete them. While you're at it, schedule some time to listen to the next Third Ear Activator: **Resolving Value Conflicts (https://soundcloud.com/nance-l-schick/resolving-personal-value-conflicts)**. In it, we look at why you never get done the things that you say are important to you.

Action One: Define the Conflict

I became a _____ because I thought it would _____.

Action Two: Identify the Interests

I want _____.

I thought _____.

I believe _____.

I expected _____.

I wish _____.

I have to _____.

Action Three: Play with the Possibilities

If I could have this conflict resolve in any way possible, _____

_____

_____

_____

_____.

Action Four: Create the Future

Three specific, measurable, individualized, likeable, and easy (SMILE) actions I can take this week:

1. I will _____ by _____ (or on _____).

2. I will _____ by _____ (or on _____).

3. I will _____ by _____ (or on _____).

Action Five: Stay on PARR

Plan, act, revise, and repeat, until you get the results you want—or something better!

VALUES CONFLICTS

Because you're still in the early stages of this Third Ear Conflict Resolution Program, let's review the Seven Choices again. Whenever you feel stuck or confused in a conflict, there's a good chance you are emotionally-charged. Come back and make these choices again before you try to engage with anyone else about this:

1. Forgive yourself for having conflicts.
2. Acknowledge yourself for taking any action to resolve any conflict.
3. Forgive the world for having conflicts.
4. Free the emotions.
5. Clear your mind.
6. Assume that you know nothing about anything.
7. Listen with your third ear.

We develop our values from a variety of sources: our families, schools, religious organizations, governments, etc. Yet most of us disagree with some of what we are told is the way we are supposed to be or with the things we are supposed to do. We think that makes us bad people, so we try to conform, and we deny life to parts of ourselves. This also shows up in our schedules, as you'll hear in my example. As always, please write the first responses that come to mind. If they came to your mind, your subconscious is trying to tell you something. There's no right or wrong, so don't judge. Just write and reflect.

Here's an example of how I resolved this conflict several years ago.

I say that I value _____, but _____.

1. **Define the conflict.** I say that I value quality time with my loved ones above all else, but I am often too busy to visit them.

2. **Identify the interests.** I want to give my undivided attention to whoever I am with. I want to do a great job on whatever I am doing. I sometimes obsess over details, and things take me longer than I expect.

3. **Play with the possibilities.** If I could have this conflict resolve in any way possible, I would have a balanced life that allowed me to do exceptional work yet still have time each day to be fully present with at least one loved person I love.

4. **Create the future.** I will work with my business coach monthly on clarifying my vision and aligning my goals and actions with my vision. Every day, I will use the Third Ear Activator: Daily Planner to improve my skills in prioritization and time management. I will schedule time daily to be with my loved ones, to call them, to email them, and to be available when unexpected needs arise. I will also schedule weekly outings, monthly visits, three to four trips per year to Kentucky, and one yearly vacation where we can play together.

What SMILE actions will you take this week to align your schedule with what you really value? Make a list of three to five steps you will take. Then, put them into your calendar and ensure you have allowed time to complete them. While you're at it, schedule some time to listen to the next Third Ear Activator: **Resolving Health Conflicts (https://soundcloud.com/nance-l-schick/resolving-health-conflicts)**. We'll be looking at why you aren't taking sufficient care of your body. In the meantime, it's your turn to complete this exercise on Values Conflicts.

Action One: Define the Conflict

I say that I value _____, but _____.

Action Two: Identify the Interests

I want _____.

I thought _____.

I believe _____.

I expected _____.

I wish _____.

I have to _____.

Action Three: Play with the Possibilities

If I could have this conflict resolve in any way possible, _____

_____

_____

_____

_____.

Action Four: Create the Future

Three SMILE actions I can take this week:

1. I will _____ by _____ (or on _____).
2. I will _____ by _____ (or on _____).
3. I will _____ by _____ (or on _____).

Action Five: Stay on PARR

Plan, act, revise, and repeat, until you get the results you want—or something better!

HEALTH CONFLICTS

I don't know a single person who doesn't have some sort of complaint about his or her body. It's no wonder, considering the obesity epidemic in many Western cultures and all of the marketing messages telling us we're not enough of something: skinny, pretty, muscular, energetic, sexual, sexy, fit, and so on. In some ways, this could be categorized as another Value Conflict, which we discussed in the last exercise. But because health is such a part of our constant conversation, I gave it a page of its own.

As always, please write the first responses that come to mind without assumptions, judgment, or a desire to punish yourself for not having the right answer. There is no right or wrong. Just write and reflect.

Here's my example.

I am too _____ to _____.

1. **Define the conflict.** I am too old to run long distances like I used to.

2. **Identify the interests.** I want to be able to run long distances, if I choose to. I want to be lean, strong, fit, and extraordinary. I want to be recognized as extraordinary. I wish I had been able to complete the New York City Marathon after all of the training I did in 2004.

3. **Play with the possibilities.** If I could have this conflict resolve in any way possible, I would be a 51-year-old with a 22-year-old body. That isn't possible. In theory, I could have multiple surgeries to look like I had a body 20 years younger, but it wouldn't actually be younger. I'd still have the degenerating joints and spine. Even if I had joint replacement surgeries, I would remain 51 years old—which is not so bad. I have a fitness level better than many 20-somethings have. I am not on any prescription medication. I have a nutrient-rich diet that keeps me energized. Life is pretty good.

4. **Create the future.** Beginning today, I will accept my age and my body as they are. Each time I pass a mirror, I will find something positive to say about the physical shell that temporarily houses my spirit. Each week, I will continue to train for longevity above all else. I will consider training for a marathon again this year, allowing myself to complete it by walking and running.

What SMILE actions will you take this week to improve your health and the way you relate to your body? Make a list of three to five steps you will take. Then, put them into your calendar and ensure you have allowed time to complete them. While you're at it, schedule some time to listen to the next Third Ear Activator: **Resolving Personal History Conflicts**. We look at how your past is ruling your future.

Here's the workspace for your Health Conflicts.

Action One: Define the Conflict

I'm too _____ to _____.

Action Two: Identify the Interests

I want _____.

I thought _____.

I believe _____.

I expected _____.

I wish _____.

I have to _____.

Action Three: Play with the Possibilities

If I could have this conflict resolve in any way possible, _____

_____

_____

_____

_____.

Action Four: Create the Future

Three SMILE actions I can take this week:

1. I will _____ by _____ (or on _____).

2. I will _____ by _____ (or on _____).

3. I will _____ by _____ (or on _____).

Action Five: Stay on PARR

Plan, act, revise, and repeat, until you get the results you want—or something better!

PERSONAL HISTORY CONFLICTS

For some of you, it can be especially painful to look at your personal history. You might have experienced something so tragic that people all around you have given you nothing but space to be angry, victimized, and weakened. You wear your experience as a badge of honor, or it provides you with a constant excuse whenever you fail to produce results in your life.

I understand. I have my own badges of honor and excuses that I have locked neatly away, but they still sometimes fall out of storage on top of my head at times, disorienting and disabling me. I am committed to ensuring that each of us masters our historical conflicts, so we get to say how our futures go.

As always, please write the first responses that come to mind without assumptions, judgment, or a desire to punish yourself for not having the right answer. There is no right or wrong. Just write and reflect.

I am _____ because when I was ____ years old, _____.

1. **Define the conflict.** I am afraid to be too vulnerable with people because I had occasional experiences of emotional, physical, sexual, and verbal abuse by people close to me from the time I was about six years old until around age 41.

2. **Identify the interests.** I wanted to be accepted. I was afraid more of being abandoned than being abused. I didn't want to bother anyone. I thought I was a bother just because I existed. I didn't think I mattered. I didn't recognize many of others' behaviors as abuse. I was embarrassed that I couldn't take care of myself and stop the abuse. I want to trust people, but my past keeps telling me not to—that they can't be trusted. I am confused because people generally occur to me as good-

natured and wanting the same things in life that I do. I suspect we all just want to be loved, even if we are ineffective in communicating that at times and under certain circumstances.

3. **Play with the possibilities.** If I could have this conflict resolve in any way possible, I would be vulnerable yet safe.

4. **Create the future.** Each day, I will fully connect with at least one person. In each moment with that person, I will be present and allow whatever conversation needs to occur do just that. In each moment, I will release the desire to control the environment. Each time I have doubt about a person, I will look for something I love about him or her. In each moment, I will trust myself to establish a boundary or leave a situation to protect my assets, my body, my soul, and my time.

What specific, measurable, individualized, likable, and easy (or SMILE) actions will you take this week to let go of or clean up your past? Make a list of three to five steps you will take. Then, put them into your calendar and ensure you have allowed time to complete them. While you're at it, schedule some time to listen to the next Third Ear Activator, which will begin a new focus on Resolving Conflicts with your Environment. We'll look at **Residence Conflicts**, **Employer Conflicts**, **Neighborhood Conflicts**, and **Citizenship Conflicts**.

Action One: Define the Conflict

I'm _____ because when I was ____ years old, _____.

Action Two: Identify the Interests

I want _____.

I thought _____.

I believe _____.

I expected _____.

I wish _____.

I have to _____.

Action Three: Play with the Possibilities

If I could have this conflict resolve in any way possible, _____

_____

_____

_____

_____.

Action Four: Create the Future

Three SMILE actions I can take this week:

1. I will _____ by _____ (or on _____).

2. I will _____ by _____ (or on _____).

3. I will _____ by _____ (or on _____).

Action Five: Stay on PARR

Plan, act, revise, and repeat, until you get the results you want—or something better!

Resolving Conflicts with Your Environment

As much as we would like to think we are self-sufficient, self-contained beings too strong to be influenced by our surroundings, we are highly sensitive to our environments. From our homes to our home countries, there is always some small change we can make to shift our experiences.

RESIDENCE CONFLICTS

Most of us have at least some control over our living situations. Not only can we practice our conflict resolution skills in our physical spaces, Feng Shui design principles suggest we can increase and channel the flow of desired energy by organizing our spaces.

If you are home right now, look around you. Is your home clean and organized? Do you have a sense of peace when you come home, or can you only see what needs to be done? Look at the walls. Are they bare and ordinary, or are they expressions of your unique existence—as you want it to be? Do you have what you need to function in your space at the highest level? A bed that you sleep well in? Heat?

Hot water? Room to store and prepare nutrient-rich meals that energize you? Storage for your favorite things, whether they are pieces of art, clothing, music, books, or sports? Do you have more than what you are using or enjoying of anything?

As a former architecture student, one of the first design concepts I learned was that form follows function. Can you see how your messy home functions as a space for a messy life, whether today or every day? It can be a vicious cycle of clutter in the mind causing clutter all around, which causes more clutter in the mind. If clutter is the result of delayed decisions, what decisions can you make today to begin molding your home into the form that allows you to function at your highest levels?

Here are the first things that came to mind when I read the following statement a few years ago.

My home isn't _____ or is too _____.

1. **Define the conflict.** My home isn't complete. It needs several repairs I can't afford to make. I haven't finished repainting. I still haven't put up new baseboards or replaced the floor in my loft. Eventually, I'll have to install air conditioning, too.

2. **Identify the interests.** I want to maximize the resale value when I am ready to sell my apartment, but I also want it to be enjoyable now for me and my guests.

3. **Play with the possibilities.** If I could have this conflict resolve in any way possible, I would find affordable ways to complete the repairs and remodeling projects this year.

4. **Create the future.** I will put money in savings every month, even if it's just $20.00. I will make one request for help this week, maybe from someone who I have given free legal services over the years. I will schedule time one weekend per month to work on the projects I can do without help.

What SMILE actions will you take this week to make your home a little more enjoyable and energizing? Paint a room a new color? Buy some new pillows? Clean? Declutter? Move?

Make a list of three to five steps you will take. Then, put them into your calendar and ensure you have allowed time to complete them.

Action One: Define the Conflict

My home isn't _____ or is too _____.

Action Two: Identify the Interests

I want _____.

I thought _____.

I believe _____.

I expected _____.

I wish _____.

I have to _____.

Action Three: Play with the Possibilities

If I could have this conflict resolve in any way possible, _____

_____

_____

_____

_____.

Action Four: Create the Future

Three SMILE actions I can take this week:

1. I will _____ by _____ (or on _____).
2. I will _____ by _____ (or on _____).
3. I will _____ by _____ (or on _____).

Action Five: Stay on PARR

Plan, act, revise, and repeat, until you get the results you want—or something better!

This was your last sample. You probably know the drill now and can take it from here. If not, **schedule your free 30-minute break-through call with me (https://calendly.com/3dear/breakthrough)**.

EMPLOYER CONFLICTS

Don't expect to jump out of bed ready to rush to work every day, after blue birds sing while dressing you in the latest fashion. But do look for alignment with your values and sufficient income to meet your obligations. Without those, you will certainly experience conflicts.

Action One: Define the Conflict

My job doesn't _____.

Action Two: Identify the Interests

I want _____.

I thought _____.

I believe _____.

I expected _____.

I wish _____.

I have to _____.

Action Three: Play with the Possibilities

If I could have this conflict resolve in any way possible, _____

_____

_____

_____

_____.

Action Four: Create the Future

Three SMILE actions I can take this week:

1. Today, I will buy *48 Days to the Work and Life You Love* by Dan Miller , who wrote the foreword to this book.
2. I will _____ by _____ (or on _____).
3. I will _____ by _____ (or on _____).

Action Five: Stay on PARR

Plan, act, revise, and repeat, until you get the results you want—or something better!

NEIGHBORHOOD CONFLICTS

After my parents divorced (when I was two years old), my mom worked hard to keep us in the modest house my sisters and I grew up in. According to many financial experts, it was probably above her means, and we sacrificed a lot to stay in it because of the high crime rate in the neighborhoods we could afford. I still prioritize safety in my neighborhood, which can be defined in a variety of ways, especially since I was assaulted so close to my home.

Action One: Define the Conflict

I am not comfortable _____ where I live.

Action Two: Identify the Interests

I want _____.

I thought _____.

I believe _____.

I expected _____.

I wish _____.

I have to _____.

Action Three: Play with the Possibilities

If I could have this conflict resolve in any way possible, _____

_____

_____

_____

_____.

Action Four: Create the Future

Three SMILE actions I can take this week:

1. I will _____ by _____ (or on _____).
2. I will _____ by _____ (or on _____).
3. I will _____ by _____ (or on _____).

Action Five: Stay on PARR

Plan, act, revise, and repeat, until you get the results you want—or something better!

CITIZENSHIP CONFLICTS

Remember in 2016, when so many Americans claimed they would move to Canada, if Donald Trump won the Presidential election? I know of no one who actually moved, but his presidency certainly raised awareness of policies and procedures people don't like. That is not always a bad thing in a democracy. Take a look at what you want changed, and let your voice be heard.

Action One: Define the Conflict

Our government doesn't _____.

Action Two: Identify the Interests

I want _____.

I thought _____.

I believe _____.

I expected _____.

I wish _____.

I have to _____.

Action Three: Play with the Possibilities

If I could have this conflict resolve in any way possible, _____

_____

_____

_____

_____.

Action Four: Create the Future

Three SMILE actions I can take this week:

1. I will _____ by _____ (or on _____).
2. I will _____ by _____ (or on _____).
3. I will _____ by _____ (or on _____).

Action Five: Stay on PARR

Plan, act, revise, and repeat, until you get the results you want—or something better!

Resolving Conflicts with Self-Sufficiency

INCOME CONFLICTS

Author Simon Sinek might have said it best. Money is fuel. When we don't have enough of it to take us where we want to go, there's a conflict. Yet some of our desire for money is based on fear, and sometimes our access to it or its equivalent is greater than we think. When I was a minor league hockey executive and agent, I often had to negotiate player contracts around salary caps. One of the ways we attracted top talent when we no longer had cash was to look at other things of value that we had access to and that players might want. Are you overlooking things of value you can leverage?

Action One: Define the Conflict

My income is stopping me from _____.

Action Two: Identify the Interests

I want _____.

I thought _____.

I believe _____.

I expected _____.

I wish _____.

I have to _____.

Action Three: Play with the Possibilities

If I could have this conflict resolve in any way possible, _____

_____

_____

_____

_____.

Action Four: Create the Future

Three SMILE actions I can take this week:

1. I will _____ by _____ (or on _____).

2. I will _____ by _____ (or on _____).

3. I will _____ by _____ (or on _____).

Action Five: Stay on PARR

Plan, act, revise, and repeat, until you get the results you want—or something better!

EXPENSE CONFLICTS

Hand-in-hand with income conflicts are expense conflicts. Stop lying to yourself. You know Financial Guru Dave Ramsey is right. At times, we all spend too much money on things we don't need with money we don't have to impress people we don't even like.

Action One: Define the Conflict

I spend too much money on _____.

Action Two: Identify the Interests

I want _____.

I thought _____.

I believe _____.

I expected _____.

I wish _____.

I have to _____.

Action Three: Play with the Possibilities

If I could have this conflict resolve in any way possible, _____

_____

_____

_____

_____.

Action Four: Create the Future

Three SMILE actions I can take this week:

1. I will _____ by _____ (or on _____).
2. I will _____ by _____ (or on _____).
3. I will _____ by _____ (or on _____).

Action Five: Stay on PARR

Plan, act, revise, and repeat, until you get the results you want—or something better!

DEBT CONFLICTS

We don't like to wait for things we want, and we will go deep in debt for the promise of a better life quickly. The problem is that we often splurge on vacations that don't last or degrees that aren't great investments, not because these can't have value, but because we aren't thinking through the full costs. Debt isn't inherently bad, but the longer you owe anyone, the less freedom you have. Start taking action today toward your freedom.

Action One: Define the Conflict

I owe _____, and it keeps me from _____.

Action Two: Identify the Interests

I want_____.

I thought _____.

I believe _____.

I expected _____.

I wish _____.

I have to_____.

Action Three: Play with the Possibilities

If I could have this conflict resolve in any way possible, _____

_____

_____

_____

_____.

Action Four: Create the Future

Three SMILE actions I can take this week:

1. I will _____ by _____ (or on _____).
2. I will _____ by _____ (or on _____).
3. I will _____ by _____ (or on _____).

Action Five: Stay on PARR

Plan, act, revise, and repeat, until you get the results you want—or something better!

CASH FLOW CONFLICTS

Did you know that a large number of small businesses fail, not because they don't have good business models or provide something of value? It's often because they don't have good cash flow systems. Keep more coming in than what goes out each month, and you're closer to success than those who forget they are no longer employees. Your checks aren't coming unless you have set your clients up to pay you on time. You teach them how to treat you, so teach them well.

Action One: Define the Conflict

I consistently struggle to pay for _____.

Action Two: Identify the Interests

I want _____.

I thought _____.

I believe _____.

I expected _____.

I wish _____.

I have to _____.

Action Three: Play with the Possibilities

If I could have this conflict resolve in any way possible, _____

_____

_____

_____

_____.

Action Four: Create the Future

Three SMILE actions I can take this week:

1. I will _____ by _____ (or on _____).
2. I will _____ by _____ (or on _____).
3. I will _____ by _____ (or on _____).

Action Five: Stay on PARR

Plan, act, revise, and repeat, until you get the results you want—or something better!

Resolving Conflicts with Time

PRIORITIES CONFLICTS

Similar to the way we become disconnected from our values, we aren't always aware of what we prioritize most or how we determine that. Once you realize it, you can say no more confidently and make sure you have time for what matters most to you.

Action One: Define the Conflict

I never have time to _____.

Action Two: Identify the Interests

I want _____.

I thought _____.

I believe _____.

I expected _____.

I wish _____.

I have to _____.

Action Three: Play with the Possibilities

If I could have this conflict resolve in any way possible, _____

_____

_____

_____

_____.

Action Four: Create the Future

Three SMILE actions I can take this week:

1. I will _____ by _____ (or on _____).

2. I will _____ by _____ (or on _____).

3. I will _____ by _____ (or on _____).

Action Five: Stay on PARR

Plan, act, revise, and repeat, until you get the results you want—or something better!

PERSONAL BOUNDARY CONFLICTS

Now that you have a better idea of what you value and how you want to prioritize, you can set better boundaries around your time, money, and energy. One of the best tools I have found for building skill in saying no is William Ury's book, *The Power of a Positive No.* Stop feeling like you've been roped into too many obligations, and learn to say no to the task, yet yes to the relationship and future opportunities more aligned with what you want.

Action One: Define the Conflict

People always _____ on or to me.

Action Two: Identify the Interests

I want _____.

I thought _____.

I believe _____.

I expected _____.

I wish _____.

I have to _____.

Action Three: Play with the Possibilities

If I could have this conflict resolve in any way possible, _____

_____

_____

_____

_____.

Action Four: Create the Future

Three SMILE actions I can take this week:

1. I will _____ by _____ (or on _____).
2. I will _____ by _____ (or on _____).
3. I will _____ by _____ (or on _____).

Action Five: Stay on PARR

Plan, act, revise, and repeat, until you get the results you want—or something better!

SELF-WORTH CONFLICTS

I'm a bit tired of the talk of Imposter Syndrome, especially when it is presented as if only certain people have it. Almost everyone I've ever asked has experienced self-worth conflicts at some point in their lives. Usually, it's when we are starting something new and still building our competence. Trust me, you can learn to do almost anything you want. You're good enough.

Action One: Define the Conflict

I'm not good enough to _____.

Action Two: Identify the Interests

I want _____.

I thought _____.

I believe _____.

I expected _____.

I wish _____.

I have to _____.

Action Three: Play with the Possibilities

If I could have this conflict resolve in any way possible, _____

_____

_____

_____

_____.

Action Four: Create the Future

Three SMILE actions I can take this week:

    1. I will _____ by _____ (or on _____).

    2. I will _____ by _____ (or on _____).

    3. I will _____ by _____ (or on _____).

Action Five: Stay on PARR

Plan, act, revise, and repeat, until you get the results you want—or something better!

COURAGE CONFLICTS

My 2021 theme is courage, so I'm in deep exploration of my own conflicts around it. I'm looking at when I became the person who sought more security and less adventure. Was that really what I wanted? Is it still? What about you? Are you ready to step out of your comfort zone and get some new results?

Action One: Define the Conflict

I'm too afraid to _____.

Action Two: Identify the Interests

I want _____.

I thought _____.

I believe _____.

I expected _____.

I wish _____.

I have to _____.

Action Three: Play with the Possibilities

If I could have this conflict resolve in any way possible, _____

_____

_____

_____

_____.

Action Four: Create the Future

Three SMILE actions I can take this week:

1. I will _____ by _____ (or on _____).

2. I will _____ by _____ (or on _____).

3. I will _____ by _____ (or on _____).

Action Five: Stay on PARR

Plan, act, revise, and repeat, until you get the results you want—or something better!

Resolving Body Conflicts

WEIGHT CONFLICTS

After the assault, as I've aged, and throughout the pandemic, I've put on a few extra pounds that stubbornly cling to me like spinach on my front tooth during a first date. I know what used to work for my body, but it has changed. So, I have to revisit this exercise frequently. I've learned to accept that and, as I am writing this, embracing it as a game I can win.

Action One: Define the Conflict

I used to weigh _____ (or be a size _____).

Action Two: Identify the Interests

I want _____.

I thought _____.

I believe _____.

I expected _____.

I wish _____.

I have to _____.

Action Three: Play with the Possibilities

If I could have this conflict resolve in any way possible, _____

_____

_____

_____

_____.

Action Four: Create the Future

Three SMILE actions I can take this week:

1. I will _____ by _____ (or on _____).

2. I will _____ by _____ (or on _____).

3. I will _____ by _____ (or on _____).

Action Five: Stay on PARR

Plan, act, revise, and repeat, until you get the results you want—or something better!

ENERGY CONFLICTS

Short and sweet: you are not a machine. You do not run on coffee, sugar, or whatever else you use to keep your energy up. Get more sleep and take more breaks. Use this exercise to explore what is stopping you from doing these.

Action One: Define the Conflict

I'm always too tired to _____.

Action Two: Identify the Interests

I want _____.

I thought _____.

I believe _____.

I expected _____.

I wish _____.

I have to _____.

Action Three: Play with the Possibilities

If I could have this conflict resolve in any way possible, _____

_____

_____

_____

_____.

Action Four: Create the Future

Three SMILE actions I can take this week:

1. I will _____ by _____ (or on _____).
2. I will _____ by _____ (or on _____).
3. I will _____ by _____ (or on _____).

Action Five: Stay on PARR

Plan, act, revise, and repeat, until you get the results you want—or something better!

BODY SHAPE CONFLICTS

This is another one that can be addressed somewhat simply. You are a unique, beautiful being. Stop comparing yourself to others and spend your time, money, and energy with people who see that. More importantly, make one of those people you. Here's an exercise to help you uncover why you aren't doing that.

Action One: Define the Conflict

My _____ is too _____ or isn't _____ enough.

Action Two: Identify the Interests

I want _____.

I thought _____.

I believe _____.

I expected _____.

I wish _____.

I have to _____.

Action Three: Play with the Possibilities

If I could have this conflict resolve in any way possible, _____

_____

_____

_____

_____.

Action Four: Create the Future

Three SMILE actions I can take this week:

1. I will _____ by _____ (or on _____).
2. I will _____ by _____ (or on _____).
3. I will _____ by _____ (or on _____).

Action Five: Stay on PARR

Plan, act, revise, and repeat, until you get the results you want—or something better!

APPEARANCE CONFLICTS

As someone who has played with hairstyles and hair colors since she was a teenager, I am not judging you for your experiments. However, I invite you to look differently at the aspects of yourself you don't like. Many people have learned to make assets what they once viewed as flaws. What hidden assets do you have?

Action One: Define the Conflict

My _____ is too _____ or isn't _____ enough.

Action Two: Identify the Interests

I want _____.

I thought _____.

I believe _____.

I expected _____.

I wish _____.

I have to _____.

Action Three: Play with the Possibilities

If I could have this conflict resolve in any way possible, _____

_____

_____

_____

_____.

Action Four: Create the Future

Three SMILE actions I can take this week:

1. I will _____ by _____ (or on _____).
2. I will _____ by _____ (or on _____).
3. I will _____ by _____ (or on _____).

Action Five: Stay on PARR

Plan, act, revise, and repeat, until you get the results you want—or something better!

Resolving Self-Image Conflicts

WARDROBE CONFLICTS

Sometimes a quick-fix like a wardrobe makeover gives us confidence to take other steps. Find your personal style and let your most powerful self shine through.

Action One: Define the Conflict

_____ always looks so _____.

Action Two: Identify the Interests

I want_____.

I thought _____.

I believe _____.

I expected _____.

I wish _____.

I have to _____.

Action Three: Play with the Possibilities

If I could have this conflict resolve in any way possible, _____

_____

_____

_____

_____.

Action Four: Create the Future

Three SMILE actions I can take this week:

1. I will _____ by _____ (or on _____).

2. I will _____ by _____ (or on _____).

3. I will _____ by _____ (or on _____).

Action Five: Stay on PARR

Plan, act, revise, and repeat, until you get the results you want—or something better!

SPEECH CONFLICTS

I go back and forth on this one. For years, I tried to hide my Kentucky accent and sound "more professional". Yet it also makes me stand out in New York. I currently think it's okay to have more than one style and to use what works in different settings. Code switching might be okay, when we're choosing it rather than feeling it is required of us.

Action One: Define the Conflict

I sound like _____.

Action Two: Identify the Interests

I want_____.

I thought _____.

I believe _____.

I expected _____.

I wish _____.

I have to _____.

Action Three: Play with the Possibilities

If I could have this conflict resolve in any way possible, _____

_____

_____

_____

_____.

Action Four: Create the Future

Three SMILE actions I can take this week:

1. I will _____ by _____ (or on _____).
2. I will _____ by _____ (or on _____).
3. I will _____ by _____ (or on _____).

Action Five: Stay on PARR

Plan, act, revise, and repeat, until you get the results you want—or something better!

WRITING CONFLICTS

I've spent a lot of time learning to write effectively, but I still hire skilled line and copy editors for my books. There is nothing wrong with getting help, if you're not a good writer. However, you can also build this skill, if you want to. If you don't that's okay, too. This exercise should help you see how important it is to you and whether it's worth your time to improve.

Action One: Define the Conflict

I'm not a good writer because _____, or I could be a better writer if _____.

Action Two: Identify the Interests

I want _____.

I thought _____.

I believe _____.

I expected _____.

I wish _____.

I have to _____.

Action Three: Play with the Possibilities

If I could have this conflict resolve in any way possible, _____

_____

_____

_____

_____.

Action Four: Create the Future

Three SMILE actions I can take this week:

1. I will _____ by _____ (or on _____).
2. I will _____ by _____ (or on _____).
3. I will _____ by _____ (or on _____).

Action Five: Stay on PARR

Plan, act, revise, and repeat, until you get the results you want—or something better!

PUBLIC IMAGE CONFLICTS

You can't control how others see you, but if you are consistently being viewed differently from how you see yourself, it might be worthwhile to see why and what you might want to change.

Action One: Define the Conflict

People always think I'm _____, and I don't understand.

Action Two: Identify the Interests

I want _____.

I thought _____.

I believe _____.

I expected _____.

I wish _____.

I have to _____.

Action Three: Play with the Possibilities

If I could have this conflict resolve in any way possible, _____

_____

_____

_____

_____.

Action Four: Create the Future

Three SMILE actions I can take this week:

1. I will _____ by _____ (or on _____).
2. I will _____ by _____ (or on _____).
3. I will _____ by _____ (or on _____).

Action Five: Stay on PARR

Plan, act, revise, and repeat, until you get the results you want—or something better!

Resolving Conflicts with the Future

FINANCIAL INVESTMENT CONFLICTS

Make no mistake thinking investments are only financial products rich people have. We invest in a variety of ways every day. We invest our time in education, relationships, and fitness. We invest in our energy levels by resting, dancing, or meditating. We live in the present, yet the choices we make in all areas are investments in our future. Nevertheless, this exercise is about money and how to ensure you are creating the financial future you want.

Action One: Define the Conflict

My investments are _____.

Action Two: Identify the Interests

I want _____.

I thought _____.

I believe _____.

I expected _____.

I wish _____.

I have to _____.

Action Three: Play with the Possibilities

If I could have this conflict resolve in any way possible, _____

_____

_____

_____

_____.

Action Four: Create the Future

Three SMILE actions I can take this week:

1. I will _____ by _____ (or on _____).

2. I will _____ by _____ (or on _____).

3. I will _____ by _____ (or on _____).

Action Five: Stay on PARR

Plan, act, revise, and repeat, until you get the results you want—or something better!

SAVINGS CONFLICTS

It is estimated that 69% of Americans have less than $1,000.00 in savings. Most experts recommend you have enough money in savings to cover three to six months of expenses. That alone is a conflict. Are you taking action to resolve this? Why not?

Action One: Define the Conflict

My savings are _____.

Action Two: Identify the Interests

I want _____.

I thought _____.

I believe _____.

I expected _____.

I wish _____.

I have to _____.

Action Three: Play with the Possibilities

If I could have this conflict resolve in any way possible, _____

_____

_____

_____

_____.

Action Four: Create the Future

Three SMILE actions I can take this week:

1. I will _____ by _____ (or on _____).
2. I will _____ by _____ (or on _____).
3. I will _____ by _____ (or on _____).

Action Five: Stay on PARR

Plan, act, revise, and repeat, until you get the results you want—or something better!

HEALTH CARE CONFLICTS

When I was assaulted in 2014, I didn't want to go to the emergency room (ER) because I had no health insurance. That probably kept me from getting better care. Fortunately, my head injury was not worse. I still bought a plan I couldn't really afford and quickly learned— while at the hospital after another head injury—it didn't cover ER visits. I spent two years paying off that bill, so I understand if you have health care conflicts. I revisit this one nearly every year.

Action One: Define the Conflict

My health care plan is _____ or doesn't cover

_____.

Action Two: Identify the Interests

I want _____.

I thought _____.

I believe _____.

I expected _____.

I wish _____.

I have to _____.

Action Three: Play with the Possibilities

If I could have this conflict resolve in any way possible, _____

_____

_____

_____

_____.

Action Four: Create the Future

Three SMILE actions I can take this week:

1. I will _____ by _____ (or on _____).
2. I will _____ by _____ (or on _____).
3. I will _____ by _____ (or on _____).

Action Five: Stay on PARR

Plan, act, revise, and repeat, until you get the results you want—or something better!

ESTATE PLANNING CONFLICTS

Few people like to think about their inevitable deaths, but they are inevitable. If you don't take the time to plan for your death, the state you live in at the time will determine for you who gets your money, home, furniture, jewelry, and so much more. This is one of the areas in which you can reclaim some power easily. The exercise below will get you thinking about how to align your estate planning with your values and desires—regardless of how much or little you have.

Action One: Define the Conflict

I don't want _____ benefiting from my death.

Action Two: Identify the Interests

I want _____.

I thought _____.

I believe _____.

I expected _____.

I wish _____.

I have to _____.

Action Three: Play with the Possibilities

If I could have this conflict resolve in any way possible, _____

_____

_____

_____

_____.

Action Four: Create the Future

Three SMILE actions I can take this week:

1. I will _____ by _____ (or on _____).
2. I will _____ by _____ (or on _____).
3. I will _____ by _____ (or on _____).

Action Five: Stay on PARR

Plan, act, revise, and repeat, until you get the results you want—or something better!

Resolving Conflicts with Everyday Life

DISTRACTIONS

One of my closest friends often reminds me that distraction is one of the most powerful tools people have to use against us. Sun Tzu, author of *The Art of War*, encouraged his readers to use the unexpected to their advantage because it keeps adversaries unprepared. Conversely, those who maintain focus on their goals will typically achieve them. Don't let others benefit unjustly because you are easily distracted. Dig in to determine what gets you off course, so you can steer yourself back until you get where you want to go.

Action One: Define the Conflict

I can't have _____ when I am working or studying.

Action Two: Identify the Interests

I want _____.

I thought _____.

I believe _____.

I expected _____.

I wish _____.

I have to _____.

Action Three: Play with the Possibilities

If I could have this conflict resolve in any way possible, _____

_____

_____

_____

_____.

Action Four: Create the Future

Three SMILE actions I can take this week:

1. I will _____ by _____ (or on _____).

2. I will _____ by _____ (or on _____).

3. I will _____ by _____ (or on _____).

Action Five: Stay on PARR

Plan, act, revise, and repeat, until you get the results you want—or something better!

NATURAL DISASTERS

Nature is going to continue to send blizzards, forest fires, hurricanes, and pandemics. It's a sad and frustrating reality that we are probably better off working around than pretending we can control. There are a number of ways to minimize your risk of future, similar harm. For now, let's work through how you were caught off guard, so we can choose the right risk management structure for you going forward.

Action One: Define the Conflict

_____ destroyed _____.

Action Two: Identify the Interests

I want _____.

I thought _____.

I believe _____.

I expected _____.

I wish _____.

I have to _____.

Action Three: Play with the Possibilities

If I could have this conflict resolve in any way possible, _____

_____

_____

_____

_____.

Action Four: Create the Future

Three SMILE actions I can take this week:

1. I will _____ by _____ (or on _____).
2. I will _____ by _____ (or on _____).
3. I will _____ by _____ (or on _____).

Action Five: Stay on PARR

Plan, act, revise, and repeat, until you get the results you want—or something better!

BREAKDOWNS

I don't always recognize it in the exact moment I become emotionally prickly, but I have learned to appreciate breakdowns because they are generally followed by breakthroughs. This is especially true when I reclaim my power and guide the process. That's why I often say, "BYOB: Bring your own breakdown."

Action One: Define the Conflict

I had a complete meltdown when _____.

Action Two: Identify the Interests

I want _____.

I thought _____.

I believe _____.

I expected _____.

I wish _____.

I have to _____.

Action Three: Play with the Possibilities

If I could have this conflict resolve in any way possible, _____

_____

_____

_____

_____.

Action Four: Create the Future

Three SMILE actions I can take this week:

1. I will _____ by _____ (or on _____).
2. I will _____ by _____ (or on _____).
3. I will _____ by _____ (or on _____).

Action Five: Stay on PARR

Plan, act, revise, and repeat, until you get the results you want—or something better!

ACCIDENTS

Disabling injuries due to accidents create a variety of conflicts, regardless of how long the impairment lasts. I tend to continue working whenever possible, but that doesn't mean it's easy or without pain. It also doesn't mean everyone can do what I do. Yet there is certainly something you can do to maintain as close a lifestyle to the one you had before the accident. Let's find that for you.

Action One: Define the Conflict

I hit/fell/hurt _____.

Action Two: Identify the Interests

I want _____.

I thought _____.

I believe _____.

I expected _____.

I wish _____.

I have to _____.

Action Three: Play with the Possibilities

If I could have this conflict resolve in any way possible, _____

_____

_____

_____

_____.

Action Four: Create the Future

Three SMILE actions I can take this week:

1. I will _____ by _____ (or on _____).
2. I will _____ by _____ (or on _____).
3. I will _____ by _____ (or on _____).

Action Five: Stay on PARR

Plan, act, revise, and repeat, until you get the results you want—or something better!

Resolving Conflicts in Relationships

FAMILY CONFLICTS

Let's be honest. Your family doesn't function seamlessly and consistently any certain way. It's comprised of individuals who agree to various roles, rules, and rituals, either expressly or through silence and acquiescence. Keep that in mind as you work through the next exercise. The ones following it will help you look more closely at the individuals that make up your family, whether given or chosen.

Action One: Define the Conflict

My family doesn't _____ or always _____.

Action Two: Identify the Interests

I want _____.

I thought _____.

I believe _____.

I expected _____.

I wish _____.

I have to _____.

Action Three: Play with the Possibilities

If I could have this conflict resolve in any way possible, _____

_____

_____

_____

_____.

Action Four: Create the Future

Three SMILE actions I can take this week:

1. I will _____ by _____ (or on _____).

2. I will _____ by _____ (or on _____).

3. I will _____ by _____ (or on _____).

Action Five: Stay on PARR

Plan, act, revise, and repeat, until you get the results you want—or something better!

PARTNER CONFLICTS

You know how people complain about their spouses or partners expecting them to read their minds? They're right. We sometimes do expect that, and it will only set us up for failure. As a lawyer, I am trained to state what is sometimes obvious to some people in the room because what isn't stated clearly will be filled in with theories and assumptions. I can't be confident they fully understand my client's position unless I tell the complete story. The same is true with my partner, although I often forget. What are you forgetting—or withholding—from your partner about what you want, need, and expect? Get ready to express yourself more clearly so you both have opportunities to improve the relationship.

Action One: Define the Conflict

My partner or spouse doesn't _____ or always

_____.

Action Two: Identify the Interests

I want _____.

I thought _____.

I believe _____.

I expected _____.

I wish _____.

I have to _____.

Action Three: Play with the Possibilities

If I could have this conflict resolve in any way possible, _____

_____

_____

_____

_____.

Action Four: Create the Future

Three SMILE actions I can take this week:

1. I will _____ by _____ (or on _____).
2. I will _____ by _____ (or on _____).
3. I will _____ by _____ (or on _____).

Action Five: Stay on PARR

Plan, act, revise, and repeat, until you get the results you want—or something better!

FRIEND CONFLICTS

Don't be surprised if this exercise and the next reveal that some of the people you thought were friends are actually more casual acquaintances and vice versa. This is good information that will help you make better choices. There's nothing wrong. Just go with it.

Action One: Define the Conflict

My friend, _____, doesn't _____ or always _____.

Action Two: Identify the Interests

I want _____.

I thought _____.

I believe _____.

I expected _____.

I wish _____.

I have to _____.

Action Three: Play with the Possibilities

If I could have this conflict resolve in any way possible, _____

_____

_____

_____

_____.

Action Four: Create the Future

Three SMILE actions I can take this week:

1. I will _____ by _____ (or on _____).
2. I will _____ by _____ (or on _____).
3. I will _____ by _____ (or on _____).

Action Five: Stay on PARR

Plan, act, revise, and repeat, until you get the results you want—or something better!

ACQUAINTANCE CONFLICTS

Notice that there are separate exercises for friends and acquaintances. It's important you learn the difference, as not every relationship has the same level of commitment. This only becomes an issue when the terms of the relationship are unclear. You don't necessarily need to ask for a detailed term sheet for every relationship. However, you are wise to assume all are acquaintanceships, until there have been discussions that clarify a deeper level of commitment and loyalty.

Action One: Define the Conflict

_____ is so _____.

Action Two: Identify the Interests

I want _____.

I thought _____.

I believe _____.

I expected _____.

I wish _____.

I have to _____.

Action Three: Play with the Possibilities

If I could have this conflict resolve in any way possible, _____

_____

_____

_____

_____.

Action Four: Create the Future

Three SMILE actions I can take this week:

1. I will _____ by _____ (or on _____).
2. I will _____ by _____ (or on _____).
3. I will _____ by _____ (or on _____).

Action Five: Stay on PARR

Plan, act, revise, and repeat, until you get the results you want—or something better!

Resolving Conflicts at Work

WORKLOAD CONFLICTS

I say I hate this conflict, but I have it a lot, which suggests I am getting something out of it. Ouch. What are you getting out of your workload conflicts? Some things I've seen in my own life from past use of this exercise are opportunities for more responsibility, more work, expressions of appreciation from my boss or clients, and the perception of importance. Not all of these are what I was seeking when I got them. I've had to build skill in asking for what I want and aligning it with what the people I work for want and need.

Action One: Define the Conflict

I have too much _____ and not enough _____.

Action Two: Identify the Interests

I want_____.

I thought _____.

I believe _____.

I expected _____.

I wish _____.

I have to_____.

Action Three: Play with the Possibilities

If I could have this conflict resolve in any way possible, _____

_____

_____

_____

_____.

Action Four: Create the Future

Three SMILE actions I can take this week:

1. I will _____ by _____ (or on _____).

2. I will _____ by _____ (or on _____).

3. I will _____ by _____ (or on _____).

Action Five: Stay on PARR

Plan, act, revise, and repeat, until you get the results you want—or something better!

WORK TYPE CONFLICTS

One of the best parts of entrepreneurship is the ability to choose what I work on and when. That isn't true 100% of the time, and business ownership isn't the only way to do this. But either way, you will need to get clear on the work you like to do, are good at, and aren't skilled in. Then, you can take appropriate action to do work that you can excel in.

Action One: Define the Conflict

I never get to _____. I am always doing _____, and I hate it.

Action Two: Identify the Interests

I want _____.

I thought _____.

I believe _____.

I expected _____.

I wish _____.

I have to _____.

Action Three: Play with the Possibilities

If I could have this conflict resolve in any way possible, _____

_____

_____

_____

_____.

Action Four: Create the Future

Three SMILE actions I can take this week:

1. I will _____ by _____ (or on _____).
2. I will _____ by _____ (or on _____).
3. I will _____ by _____ (or on _____).

Action Five: Stay on PARR

Plan, act, revise, and repeat, until you get the results you want—or something better!

WORK DISTRIBUTION CONFLICTS

If you had siblings in the house with you when you were growing up, you probably had this conflict for the first time at an early age. If it wasn't resolved effectively and completely, don't be surprised when it shows up throughout your adult life. Are you ready to let that go?

Action One: Define the Conflict

_____ is always doing _____ while I am stuck _____.

Action Two: Identify the Interests

I want _____.

I thought _____.

I believe _____.

I expected _____.

I wish _____.

I have to _____.

Action Three: Play with the Possibilities

If I could have this conflict resolve in any way possible, _____

_____

_____

_____

_____.

Action Four: Create the Future

Three SMILE actions I can take this week:

1. I will _____ by _____ (or on _____).
2. I will _____ by _____ (or on _____).
3. I will _____ by _____ (or on _____).

Action Five: Stay on PARR

Plan, act, revise, and repeat, until you get the results you want—or something better!

WORK EFFECTIVENESS CONFLICTS

Is your boss a jerk, are you not doing your best, or is it something else? I've been on both sides of this conflict, and I've mediated several conflicts like it. Sometimes your employer didn't know exactly what was needed for your job and chose you, not realizing you lacked some of the most desired skills. At other times, you oversold yourself and thought you could fake it until you made it. Regardless of why you don't feel effective at work, there's a fix. It might not look the way you expect it to, but there are always a few actions you can take to resolve the issues for everyone involved.

Action One: Define the Conflict

_____ is never satisfied with what I do.

Action Two: Identify the Interests

I want _____.

I thought _____.

I believe _____.

I expected _____.

I wish _____.

I have to _____.

Action Three: Play with the Possibilities

If I could have this conflict resolve in any way possible, _____

_____

_____

_____

_____.

Action Four: Create the Future

Three SMILE actions I can take this week:

1. I will _____ by _____ (or on _____).
2. I will _____ by _____ (or on _____).
3. I will _____ by _____ (or on _____).

Action Five: Stay on PARR

Plan, act, revise, and repeat, until you get the results you want—or something better!

Resolving Conflicts with Vendors

VENDOR PERFORMANCE CONFLICTS

You might not always think of them this way, but everyone you purchase goods or services from is a vendor. You rely on some more than others, and a few of them provide things so value to you that you have a hard time imagining life without them—at least until there's a blackout, a car accident, or some other disruptive event. Dependence puts you in a weaker bargaining position, so let's look at how to ask for what you need from your vendors and walk away more powerfully, if you can't get it.

Action One: Define the Conflict

_____ didn't _____.

Action Two: Identify the Interests

I want _____.

I thought _____.

I believe _____.

I expected _____.

I wish _____.

I have to _____.

Action Three: Play with the Possibilities

If I could have this conflict resolve in any way possible, _____

_____

_____

_____

_____.

Action Four: Create the Future

Three SMILE actions I can take this week:

1. I will _____ by _____ (or on _____).

2. I will _____ by _____ (or on _____).

3. I will _____ by _____ (or on _____).

Action Five: Stay on PARR

Plan, act, revise, and repeat, until you get the results you want—or something better!

VENDOR INVOICE CONFLICTS

I grew up in a household where we watered down Campbell's soup and split it among four people for dinner. We didn't leave the lights on, let the water run, or waste much of anything. Every penny counted and still does. So, one way to lose my business is to over-charge me. This is more common than ever, due to automatic payments, and I'm learning to speak up earlier and more often. Are you?

Action One: Define the Conflict

_____ charged me $_____ for _____!

Action Two: Identify the Interests

I want _____.

I thought _____.

I believe _____.

I expected _____.

I wish _____.

I have to _____.

Action Three: Play with the Possibilities

If I could have this conflict resolve in any way possible, _____

_____

_____

_____

_____.

Action Four: Create the Future

Three SMILE actions I can take this week:

1. I will _____ by _____ (or on _____).
2. I will _____ by _____ (or on _____).
3. I will _____ by _____ (or on _____).

Action Five: Stay on PARR

Plan, act, revise, and repeat, until you get the results you want—or something better!

VENDOR QUALITY CONFLICTS

I love supporting small businesses, especially those that provide amazing and individualized products and services. But sometimes I have to buy from the huge retailer that puts 1/1,000,000th value on my purchase. I don't like that my money means so little, and I take some of my power back by considering my purchases more carefully (and spending less). How do you handle the reduction in quality? Why?

Action One: Define the Conflict

My _____ still doesn't or isn't _____, but at least it's

_____.

Action Two: Identify the Interests

I want _____.

I thought _____.

I believe _____.

I expected _____.

I wish _____.

I have to _____.

Action Three: Play with the Possibilities

If I could have this conflict resolve in any way possible, _____

_____

_____

_____

_____.

Action Four: Create the Future

Three SMILE actions I can take this week:

1. I will _____ by _____ (or on _____).
2. I will _____ by _____ (or on _____).
3. I will _____ by _____ (or on _____).

Action Five: Stay on PARR

Plan, act, revise, and repeat, until you get the results you want—or something better!

VENDOR COMMUNICATION CONFLICTS

Do you sometimes feel like you must be speaking a foreign language to your vendor? You call for help logging into your account or fixing a service issue, and you get a solution for a different problem. Then, the vendor representative acts like you are being unreasonable. Perhaps before you make that request for service, you can do a quick analysis of exactly what you want and need. This will help you be more direct with your requests. According to Brené Brown in *Dare to Lead*, clarity is kindness. So, you can be direct and still use your third ear.

Action One: Define the Conflict

I specifically said _____, but _____ did (or gave me) _____.

Action Two: Identify the Interests

I want _____.

I thought _____.

I believe _____.

I expected _____.

I wish _____.

I have to _____.

Action Three: Play with the Possibilities

If I could have this conflict resolve in any way possible, _____

_____

_____

_____

_____.

Action Four: Create the Future

Three SMILE actions I can take this week:

1. I will _____ by _____ (or on _____).
2. I will _____ by _____ (or on _____).
3. I will _____ by _____ (or on _____).

Action Five: Stay on PARR

Plan, act, revise, and repeat, until you get the results you want—or something better!

Resolving Conflicts with Revenue

BRANDING CONFLICTS

The subtitle of Tony A. Gaskins, Jr.'s book *The Dream Chaser* reads, "If You Don't Build Your Dream, Someone Will Hire You to Help Build Theirs". This is true for entrepreneurs, too. When we don't know where we want to go, what our unique selling proposition (USP) is, or how to communicate it effectively, we are at huge risk of following someone else's blueprint and wondering why we didn't get the custom design we wanted. Take the time to do your marketing research and accept that the market will change, often quite rapidly, as we saw during the COVID-19 pandemic.

Action One: Define the Conflict

People think I am _____ or that I can't _____.

Action Two: Identify the Interests

I want _____.

I thought _____.

I believe _____.

I expected _____.

I wish _____.

I have to _____.

Action Three: Play with the Possibilities

If I could have this conflict resolve in any way possible, _____

_____

_____

_____

_____.

Action Four: Create the Future

Three SMILE actions I can take this week:

1. I will _____ by _____ (or on _____).

2. I will _____ by _____ (or on _____).

3. I will _____ by _____ (or on _____).

Action Five: Stay on PARR

Plan, act, revise, and repeat, until you get the results you want—or something better!

VALUATION CONFLICTS

When you're first moving from employee to entrepreneur, you will often think about your income in terms of time spent in exchange for an hourly pay rate. That's not how value really works, so stop doing that in your employment settings, too. You might still get paid an hourly rate, but base that rate on the value you provide to the client or employer. Negotiate accordingly. Sometimes, there are bonuses and perquisites, or "perks", available to increase the value of your compensation package. Don't be greedy and expect others to hurt so you can have more, but do demand fair compensation.

Action One: Define the Conflict

I can only charge or get paid $_____ per hour / per year for my work.

Action Two: Identify the Interests

I want _____.

I thought _____.

I believe _____.

I expected _____.

I wish _____.

I have to _____.

Action Three: Play with the Possibilities

If I could have this conflict resolve in any way possible, _____

_____

_____

_____

_____.

Action Four: Create the Future

Three SMILE actions I can take this week:

1. I will _____ by _____ (or on _____).

2. I will _____ by _____ (or on _____).

3. I will _____ by _____ (or on _____).

Action Five: Stay on PARR

Plan, act, revise, and repeat, until you get the results you want—or something better!

NETWORKING CONFLICTS

My clients, especially in the entertainment and sports industries, have often talked about getting their big breaks. Guess how many have been able to describe what that big break would be. If you guessed zero, none, or zilch, you are correct. Have you been waiting for your big break? How would that play out? Work through this exercise to see, and let me know (mailto:nancy@3dearlisteners.com?subject=My Big Break) what you discover.

Action One: Define the Conflict

If I could just meet or get an interview with _____, I could _____.

Action Two: Identify the Interests

I want_____.

I thought _____.

I believe _____.

I expected _____.

I wish _____.

I have to _____.

Action Three: Play with the Possibilities

If I could have this conflict resolve in any way possible, _____

_____

_____

_____

_____.

Action Four: Create the Future

Three SMILE actions I can take this week:

1. I will _____ by _____ (or on _____).
2. I will _____ by _____ (or on _____).
3. I will _____ by _____ (or on _____).

Action Five: Stay on PARR

Plan, act, revise, and repeat, until you get the results you want—or something better!

COMPLETION CONFLICTS

Are you putting off life experiences you want because you haven't completed something else first? Reconsider whether you have to earn the life you want by finishing something else first, especially when that other task or project might not be consistent with your values. Play with the possibilities that you already deserve what you want and have many more options than you thought.

Action One: Define the Conflict

When I finish _____, I'll make more money.

Action Two: Identify the Interests

I want _____.

I thought _____.

I believe _____.

I expected _____.

I wish _____.

I have to _____.

Action Three: Play with the Possibilities

If I could have this conflict resolve in any way possible, _____

_____

_____

_____

_____.

Action Four: Create the Future

Three SMILE actions I can take this week:

1. I will _____ by _____ (or on _____).
2. I will _____ by _____ (or on _____).
3. I will _____ by _____ (or on _____).

Action Five: Stay on PARR

Plan, act, revise, and repeat, until you get the results you want—or something better!

* * *

Speaking of completion, that was the last sample exercise.

For more exercises and tools, visit my **website** (**https://3dearcoaching.com**) regularly and **subscribe** to my monthly newsletter.

Acknowledgments

I often think of myself as a lone ranger, which leaves me feeling alone and overwhelmed. If I had not been surrounded and supported by people who know this about me, this book might not have been written for *another* eight years! Thank you, George Rylander, Tracy Frierman, Tim Vanini, Mykel Dicus, Eric Grigoriew, Peter Schmitz, Nina Kaufman, Jeri Quinn, Lisa Murdy, and Wendi Hoagland, for reaching out when I tried to hide and for giving me the pushes I needed when I got stopped.

Thank you, Steve Miller, Jerry Orange, Arielle Guy, Judy Ridolfino, Nina Kaufman, Conna Craig, and Tyler O'Keeffe, for your helpful feedback on the various drafts it took to get this book done. Thank you, Judy Cullins, for streamlining that process.

Thank you, Shirlee Hart, Jennifer Dean, Jeanette Epplein, Roberta Lipp, Wendi Hoagland, Steve Miller, Jerry Orange, Jennifer Wilkov, Nina Kaufman, Peter Schmitz, and Judy Cullins, for your assistance in choosing a title.

Thank you to all the prior employees and contractors who contributed in various forms to the development of the Third Ear Conflict Resolution Program, this book, the audio program, the app, and all the supplemental tools that make practice easier. Lia Araujo, Jennifer Dean, Candice Oden, Sherie Arnold, Brandon Walker, Farah Zubair,

Jurgen Qesari, Janet Anderton, and Sarah Cotton, we finally did this and will make a difference in people's lives!

Thank you to my mother, Anita Paulin; my sister, Lisa Coder; my nephew, Justin Paulin; my cousins, Sandy and Duke Chisholm; Tony Schick; the many, many Hartlages; and the colleagues and friends who don't always understand me but who love and support me anyway.

Thank you to the clients who have trusted me and shared their stories so I could empower people like them.

Thank you to all who doubted me. You triggered my competitiveness and desire to prove you wrong, which helped me finish this project.

Thank you, Wendi Hoagland, for being my best friend for more than thirty-three years. You taught me how to receive unconditional love, which gave me access to giving it and improving all my relationships. We've shared laughs and tears, triumphs, and tragedies. I continue to be amazed that our already exceptional friendship gets better every day.

Likewise, Peter Schmitz, I committed to re-creating my love for you each day, and I keep seeing more to love. Thank you for being my playmate, my partner, my assistant, my chief technology officer, and whatever else I need you to be. You don't let me give up, nor will I let you.

I didn't name everyone. That would be a book in itself. Don't let a missing name diminish the value of your contribution. In my fifty-one years, I've had a lot of help, for which I am grateful. I benefit from the doormen and cashiers who always greet me, the vendors who consistently deliver reliable service, the teachers who encouraged me, and even those who said I would never make it. I am humbled by all of you, and I hope I have created something of value for you.

Made in the USA
Middletown, DE
29 August 2021